THE
GOSPEL
ACCORDING TO
C·A·S·E·Y

For Brooks and Dolly

THE
GOSPEL
ACCORDING TO
C·A·S·E·Y

*Casey Stengel's
Inimitable, Instructional, Historical
Baseball Book*

IRA BERKOW AND JIM KAPLAN

ST. MARTIN'S PRESS
NEW YORK

Design by Robert Bull Design

Library of Congress Cataloging-in-Publication Data

Kaplan, Jim.
    The gospel according to Casey : Casey Stengel's inimitable,
instructional, historical baseball book / Jim Kaplan and Ira Berkow.
        p.   cm.
    "A Thomas Dunne book."
    ISBN 0-312-06922-7
    1. Stengel, Casey.   2. Baseball—United States—Managers—
Biography.   3. Baseball—Philosophy.   I. Berkow, Ira.   II. Title.
GV865. S8K37   1992
796.357′092—dc20   91-37842
[B]   CIP

First Edition: March 1992

10 9 8 7 6 5 4 3 2 1

CONTENTS

(IRA BERKOW)

(NATIONAL BASEBALL LIBRARY, COOPERSTOWN, N

(NBL)

(NBL)

INTRODUCTION

By Ira Berkow

T HE FIRST TIME I saw Casey Stengel in person was in a dugout before an old-timers' game at Shea Stadium, in July of 1968. He had come not to play but as a special guest, a former manager of the Amazin' Mets, as he called them. He was then seventy-eight, he said, though one record book disagreed, and stated he was seventy-nine. No matter, he looked ancient, like a wizened sage, who could say something profound, but then add a stage wink to remind you that there was humor at the end of the tunnel. Someone once described the late Senator Everett Dirksen of Illinois as having a stained-glass voice. If that were so, then Casey's voice was cracked stained-glass. And his syntax was cloudy but as compelling as rubbings from old churchyard tombstones.

When someone asked him about the lack of hitting in the major leagues then, he said, "They ask you, you ask yourself, I ask you, it's them good young pitchers between eighteen and twenty-four that can throw the ball over the plate and don't kill the manager, isn't it?"

Stengel's white hair, still plentiful, was sun-tinged in spots, and a wave fell across the side of his face, which was wrinkled like a rutted road. His expressive white eyebrows shaded blue eyes that watered now and then, and he wiped his eyes with a handkerchief as large as a hand towel. His tasteful blue suit was specked with light brown, and looked almost natty on him. His hands and gnarled fingers had a kind of grace when making a point that one might expect from a symphony conductor.

And his legs. Of course, his warped old legs. He crossed them at the knee and one foot worked nervously under black executive socks. On his feet were black slippers—he had been suffering pain in the lower extremities. Before ever knowing very much about Casey Stengel, I knew about his legs. I remember reading Damon Runyon's account of old Casey Stengel—he was thirty-three (or thirty-four), but seemed elderly even then—scoring an inside-the-park home run in the ninth inning of the first game of the 1923 World Series, to give his Giants a 5–4 win over the Yankees:

> "This is the way old 'Casey' Stengel ran yesterday afternoon, running his home run home . . .
>
> "His mouth wide open.
>
> "His warped old legs bending beneath him at every stride.
>
> "His arms flying back and forth like those of a man swimming with a crawl stroke.
>
> "His flanks heaving, his breath whistling, his head far back. . . ."

Three thousand miles away in California, Edna Lawson, Stengel's fiancée, had proudly showed newspaper clippings of Casey's game-winning blow to her father.

"What do you think of my Casey?" she asked.

Her father shook his head. "I hope," he said, "that your Casey lives until the wedding."

He did, of course, and well beyond. ("For the bridegroom," Casey said when they wed, "it is the best catch he ever made in his career.")

With the others who gathered around Casey in the dugout, I listened, and laughed. But also on that first afternoon that I saw him, I realized something that I had never quite appreciated. The man made some of the most interesting, original, and thoughtful comments on baseball strategy and technique that I'd ever heard, and said it in the most entertaining fashion.

He spoke then, as he would on other occasions, about players he played with or against, from Babe Ruth to Walter Johnson, and about those he managed, from Van Lingle Mungo to Joe DiMaggio and Mickey Mantle, and those he managed against, from Dizzy Dean to Jackie Robinson. Stengel is in the Hall of Fame, having managed the Yankees to ten pennants and seven World Series titles in twelve years. He managed great players in those years, from 1949 to 1960. But he also had managed some terrible teams, like the Brooklyn Dodgers in the mid-1930s, the Boston Bees (later named the Braves) in the late '30s and early '40s, and the expansion Mets of the early 1960s.

Warren Spahn, who pitched under Casey for the 1942 Braves and the 1965 Mets, said, "I played for Casey before and after he was a genius."

Casey would be the first to agree that, as he said, "it was the players that made me what I am." For good or for bad. But he also was an outstanding handler of men, a brilliant teacher, as former players attest, and an inspiration to future outstanding managers who played for him, such as Billy Martin, Whitey Herzog, and Roger Craig.

In 1974 I had written and published—with Walt Frazier of the New York Knicks, then one of basketball's best and most creative players—a rather off-beat instructional book complete with photographs and illustrations titled, *Rockin' Steady: A Guide to Basketball and Cool.* I thought that it would be a terrific thing if I could do the same with Casey Stengel, and call it *Casey Stengel's Inimitable, Instructional, Historical Baseball Book.*

I knew Casey was coming into New York for the annual dinner of the New York chapter of the Baseball Writers' Association of America, and so made an appointment to see him in his hotel room. It was late January, 1974. I remember that we talked about numerous baseball subjects, and at one point, to demonstrate a particular play, he got up from his chair—he was now eighty-four years old, more or less—and with his bowed, lumpy legs chased down an imaginary ground ball that bounced under the coffee table.

I remember his telling me about one of the most prominent players of the day, who, the next season, would break Babe Ruth's record for career home runs: "Now this fellow in Atlanta is amazin'. He hits the ball the best for a man of his size. But I can't say he hits the ball better than Ruth. Ruth could hit the ball so far nobody could field it. And that's even with the medicinal improvements today. They come along now with the aluminum cup and it improves players who only used to wear a belt and it's better for catching ground balls."

We talked about language. He said, "Today I make speeches all over. People ask me, 'Casey, how can you speak so much when you don't talk English too good?' Well, I've been invited to Europe and I say, they don't speak English over there too good, either."

I got around to telling him about my proposed book in some detail, and I also showed him *Rockin' Steady.* He took the book in his old hands and turned the large-sized, glossy pages packed with color, with great care and interest. When he got to the end and closed the book, he said, "It's a perfection thing." I took that to mean he liked it. I was delighted.

"Will you do it then, Casey?" I asked.

"Let me think about it," he said. "I'll let you know."

His word was good. He did let me know, writing to me at my office—I was then the sports editor and sports columnist for Newspaper Enterprise Association. His letter arrived about two weeks after we had met. It was written in a firm but uneven hand on lined notebook paper. The letter was in blue ink, though the envelope was written in green ink. The envelope, which was personal stationery, announced at the top left:

Casey Stengel
1663 Grandview
Glendale, California 91201

The letter read exactly as follows:

Dear Ira:

Your conversations; and the fact you were the working Writer were inthused with the Ideas was Great but frankly do not care for the great amount of work for myself.

;Sorry but am not interested. Have to many propositions otherwise for this coming season.
Fact cannot disclose my Future affairs.
Good luck.
(signed) Casey Stengel
N.Y. Mets & Hall of Famer.

It wasn't quite the answer I was hoping for—though otherwise I loved the letter (still do, and of course have saved it). I thought perhaps I'd get a chance to talk with him again about the project, but he died before that could happen, later that following year.

The idea for that book, however, stayed with me. One morning in 1989 I was having breakfast with my friend Jim Kaplan, the highly respected baseball writer, author, and former *Sports Illustrated* staffer. I happened to mention the Stengel idea, and Jim loved it. He said he'd be willing to work on it with me. We agreed to keep it Casey's book, and keep it as close as possible to the idea that Casey had considered.

Though Casey said he "frankly" didn't "care for the great amount of work" for himself, we determined that he wouldn't have minded our doing it for him. Casey, to quote one of his favorite phrases, had "done splendid." Our hope was to capture some of that splendor.

New York City
September 1, 1991

Ira Berkow,
Sports Editor,
NEA Newspaper
N.Y. City, N.Y.

Dear Ira:

Your conversations,
and the fact you were the
working writer were inthused
with the Ideas was great but
frankly do not care for the
great amount of work for myself.

Sorry but am not interested.
Have to many propositions
otherwise for this coming
season.
Fact cannot disclose my
Future affairs,
Good Luck,
Casey Stengel
N.Y. Mets & Hall of Famer,

NOTE ON ACCURACY

How much of the Casey Stengel legend is fact, and how much is, well, legend?

We found some inaccuracies in long-accepted Stengel stories. According to one, on Stengel's birthday he told the Mets' poor-fielding first baseman, Marvelous Marv Throneberry: "I was going to give you a cake, but I figured you'd drop it."

Nice line, but Throneberry told us it was actually his. "They gave Casey a cake between games of a doubleheader. I said, 'They were going to give me a cake too, but they were afraid I'd drop it.' It came out in the press that he said it." Ever the good sport, Throneberry allowed the popular version to become history. Until, that is, we forced the truth out of him.

There's another story about then–Dodger manager Stengel coming to the mound in Philadelphia's Baker Bowl to remove pitcher Boom-Boom Beck. Infuriated by the skipper's decision, Beck wheeled around and fired the ball to deepest right field. It clanged off the tin fence next to the spot where right fielder Hack Wilson, possibly hung over, was leaning with his eyes closed. Assuming the ball had been batted to him, Wilson nimbly fielded it and threw a strike to Tony Cuccinello at second base.

Another nice story, but slightly inaccurate. The Dodgers' catcher, Al Lopez, told us that he, not Stengel, had gone to the mound on Casey's advice ("Hey, Al, that's enough"). Nonetheless, Beck did fire the ball to right, and Wilson did field it and throw to second. And we have every reason to believe that Stengel did, as reported, say that Wilson's throw was the best play he made all season.

And how about these two differing stories Casey told on himself?

"One place I played they had an insane asylum—that's right, a crazy house—right outside the center-field fence, and they used to watch us play. Now I figured out, how many times do you come in from the outfield and go back out in a game, right? Every inning, that's right, that's eighteen times both ways. So I figured I could practice my sliding eighteen times every game by sliding into second base on my way out and my way in. It didn't interfere with the game, did it? Well, the loonies loved it and the people in the stands kept sayin', 'Look who's out and who's in'—but I learned slidin'."

Compare this to the story he told about taking fielding practice on the same field:

"After catching the ball and throwing it back, I'd drop my glove on the ground and slide into it while my helper got ready to hit another fly. . . . They thought I was nuts. One of the guys said the man with the butterfly nets would come for me and I'd wind up in the mental institution behind the center-field fence."

Now it's possible that Stengel was telling at least one tall tale here. Or just not remembering accurately, since a good deal of time had passed. But Casey had an excellent memory for everything but names. So it's every bit as likely that both versions are credible. Stengel worked very hard on his sliding, and he wasn't too self-conscious to practice it every chance he got.

When managing the Toledo Mud Hens in 1929, Casey noticed some players reading the stock-market page during a team meeting. According to the popular account, he told them, "I got a market tip for you. Buy all the Pennsylvania Railroad stock you can lay a hold of, and all the Baltimore & Ohio. Because when we start shipping you boys back to the bushes next week, those railroads are gonna get rich."

However, in his autobiography, *Casey at the Bat*, Stengel tells a longer, less quotable account using "Santa Fe" instead of Pennsylvania or Baltimore & Ohio.

Yet we're more inclined to believe the first version. Chances are, the more time passed, the less precise his account became. Wouldn't Toledo players be more likely to ride the Pennsylvania than Santa Fe line? But a put-down in either version is quintessential Stengelese.

Sometimes two reporters in the same room seem to have scribbled down different versions of this Stengelese. During the last three weeks of the 1951 pennant race, the old catcher Lopez, now the Cleveland manager, decided to use a three-man rotation consisting of his aces Early Wynn, Bob Lemon, and Mike Garcia. Stengel was quoted as saying, "Well, yes, I see where he's doing that. They say you can never do that, but he is, and it's a good idea but sometimes it doesn't always work."

That rather thoughtful statement may have been shortened in another report to "I've always heard it couldn't be done, but sometimes it don't always work." A nifty bit of Stengelese for the ages, but sometimes he don't always talk that way.

Unless he made both statements on different occasions. That's more a probability than a possibility to Stengel biographer Maury Allen. When Stengel and Allen saw singer Robert Goulet performing in St. Louis, Allen quoted Casey as saying, "He has feminine appeal, just like me." Another published version quoted Stengel saying, "He has effeminate appeal, just like me."

"He probably said it both ways," says Allen, "and it could have just been reported both ways. Sometimes you weren't able to hear exactly what he said.

"But there was no exaggerating Casey's legend," according to Allen. "Unlike Yogi Berra's, which was based on malaprops, Casey was absolutely legitimate."

—Jim Kaplan

(UPI/BETTMANN)

DISCOURSE ON STENGELESE

OR

"Now Wait a Minute," by the Professor Himself.

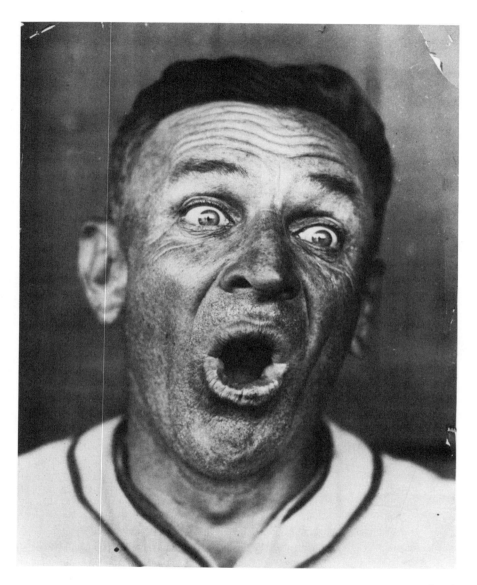

WHEN CASEY STENGEL TALKED, he fractured syntax and funny bone alike. Without stopping for breath, he'd begin stories with the Socratic "Why wouldn't ya wanna . . . ?," detour several times, lapse into anecdote and opinion, dangle a few participles, split a few infinitives, never quite introduce a pronoun to an antecedent, interrupt his interrupters ("Now wait a minute, that's what I been tryin' to tell ya"), and conclude with fresh insights about the original point. Some observers felt he used Stengelese to avoid answering tough questions. Others insisted his endless monologues were just Casey thinking aloud. Stengel (he was probably nicknamed Casey because he came from Kansas City, or K.C.) himself wrote that his language may have become contorted the day one Mrs. Kennedy made the young southpaw write righthanded in grammar school. He also may have been influenced by vaudeville performers in his hometown of Kansas City, Missouri. Many of Casey's comments were incisive, some were labyrinthine, most were gems, and quite a few became American classics. "My god," said a reporter hearing Casey for the first time, "he talks the way James Joyce writes."

THE EARLY YEARS (1890–1925)

[Reflecting on a minor-league game he played]
I made six hits and a couple of tremendous catches in the outfield. I am so fast I overrun one base and am tagged out. I steal a couple of bases, which is embarrassing for me because there's already runners on them.

It used to be that you had to catch the ball two-handed because the glove was so small. Why, when I got married I couldn't afford dress gloves, so I wore my baseball mitt to my wedding and nobody even noticed. That took care of my

3

right hand, and I was smart enough to keep my left hand in my pocket.

They brought me up to the Brooklyn Dodgers, which at that time was in Brooklyn.

[Reaction to being traded from the Phillies to the Giants in 1921]
Wake up, muscles, we're in New York now.

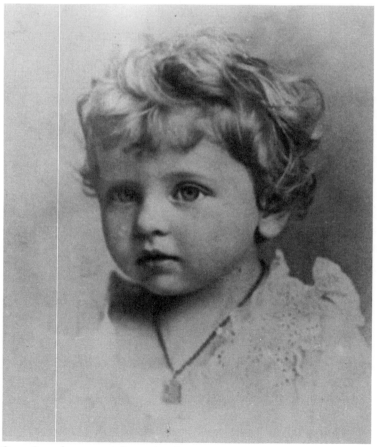

Casey Stengel as a young boy.   (NBL)

The King of England greets Casey Stengel, 1924. (NBL)

The higher-ups complained I wasn't showing a serious attitude by hiding a sparrow in my hat, but I said any day I got three hits, I figure I am showing a more serious attitude than a lot of players with no sparrow in their hats.

[Why he didn't slide home in a game as a Pirate]
With the salary I get here, I'm so hollow and starving that I'm liable to explode like a light bulb if I hit the ground too hard.

When I played in Brooklyn, I could go to the ballpark for a nickel carfare. But now I live in Pasadena, and it costs me fifteen or sixteen dollars to take a cab to Glendale. If I was a young man, I'd study to become a cabdriver.

FIRST MANAGING: CASEY WITH MINOR-LEAGUE AND LOSING MAJOR-LEAGUE TEAMS (1926–48)

It's like I used to tell my barber. Shave and a haircut but don't cut my throat. I may want to do that myself.

[When a scout told Stengel, then managing the Oakland Oaks, about a young pitcher who had allowed a single foul ball while pitching a no-hitter]
Get the guy that got the foul. It's hitters we need, not pitchers.

[On the batting stances used by Cubs second baseman Billy Herman]
He's an unusual hitter. Sometimes he stands straight up, and sometimes his head is so close to the plate he looks like John the Baptist.

[Asked to keep pitcher Van Lingle Mungo from jumping the Dodgers]
Let 'im go. I can lose with or without him.

"Just keep talking. When a newspaperman comes around, don't try to feed him some particular story. Chances are it'd be nothing he could use. Just keep talking and he'll get his story."
—Ring Lardner, advising Casey in 1934

Wherever I go, they throw in a bridge as part of the service. Every manager wants to jump off a bridge sooner or later, and it is very nice for an old man like me to know he don't have to walk fifty miles to find one.

[After his Dodgers knocked the Giants out of the 1934 pennant race on the last weekend of the season]
The Giants thought we gave 'em a beating Saturday and yesterday. Well, they were right. But I'm sorry for them when I think of the beating they still have to take. Wait till their wives realize they're not going to get those new fur coats. I've been through it, and I know.

WITH THE YANKEES (1949–60)

I never had so many good players before. I'm with a lot of real pros. When I think of some of those other teams I had, I was wondering whether I was managing a baseball team or a golf course. You know what I mean—one pro to a club.

[Returning from being hospitalized with chest pains during the 1960 season]
They examined all my organs. Some of them are quite remarkable and others are not so good. A lot of museums are bidding for them.

[When asked if Don Larsen's perfect game was the best game he had ever seen him pitch]
So far.

Stengel's home at Glendale, California, is right out of a movie set. Swimming pool, tennis courts, and all the other falderals without which no California home is considered complete. On the alabaster-white ceiling of his living room is a heel print, which is as out of place as a Broadway columnist in a church. And what do you suppose is the reason for this defacement? Casey, who acts out every story he tells— and he tells 'em as long as his listeners can stand—told me about the kicking ability of Morley Drury, who played fullback for Southern California in the days when Southern California was a football team and not a geographical description. Stengel, to show his guests how Drury could kick, punted himself and lost a shoe in the effort. Mrs. Stengel, a charming lady, in the vain hope that the telltale mark might reform Casey, allowed it to remain imprinted on the ceiling. The mark remains unchanged, and so does Casey. . . .
" 'If he does not quit baseball this year I'm going to leave him,' insisted Mrs. Casey Stengel yesterday [February 21, 1952], 'and I want you to put that in the paper too . . .' "
" 'For twenty-seven years all I've heard is baseball talk. This boy can't go to his right. That boy can't hit a curveball. You can run on this fellow. You can pitch to that fellow. One man is a Kraut Head, another is a Road Apple, and another is a Fancy Dan and last year I heard all about switch hitters because Mickey Mantle was on the team. If just once in a while we had some other topic of conversation around the house. Even a good messy ax murder.' "
                                                            —The Joe Williams Reader

"Stengel was noted for having an incredible memory, except for one blind spot. Names of people. He often mixed them up. Herb Norman remembers that when he and Stengel began working together, the old manager kept calling him 'Logan.'

"After a month, Norman went into Stengel's office. 'Casey,' he said, 'my name is not Logan. My name is Herb Norman.'

"Stengel looked at him with that gnarled, gremlin face, and said, 'Do I make my checks out right for you?' "

—IRA BERKOW, Newspaper Enterprise Association, September 14, 1976

"He had a lot of people to communicate with. He would say, 'that big guy' or 'the lefthander' because he was more concerned with the points he was making than the names. There's got to be a lot of small talk before an idea comes out. When I was the Tigers' pitching coach, I loved to talk about airplane flying with Denny McLain and Mickey Lolich. I would talk to them about these things and get around to pitching later. I read a book about brainstorming. It said that you should be encouraged to talk about anything, and then an idea comes out."

—JOHNNY SAIN

"He was called the Professor or Old Perfesser because he loved to lecture sports-writers. You'd be out three or four hours before the game and you'd find him on the bench. He'd talk to anyone: groundkeepers, young players.

"He had an uncanny memory for faces but couldn't remember names. He would say, 'the big lefthander who hit home runs' when he meant Ruth and 'the big righthander who could whistle it by you' when he meant Walter Johnson.

"The doubletalking was mostly a public act, because he could talk straight in private. He doubletalked in part to diffuse pinpoint questions. If you asked him who he was going to start at second base, he'd doubletalk because he wouldn't want to decide until he made out his lineup ten minutes before the game. But he had a way of alerting the regular beat writers. If he veered off into talking about Rogers Hornsby, you knew he wanted an offensive second baseman for a high-scoring game. That meant Billy Martin. If he mentioned a good defensive player from years past, he wanted one for a low-scoring game. That meant Jerry Coleman, who could field better than Martin."

—MAURY ALLEN

[On players' wives]
Keep them apart and help the club.

"After I hit a home run in the ninth inning to win the first game of the 1949 World Series, 1–0, a reporter afterward recalled to Casey that in the third game of the 1923 World Series he had hit a home run in the seventh inning to win the

game, 1–0. 'But Casey,' the reporter said, 'how come you didn't hit yours in the ninth inning, too?' Casey said, 'Couldn't wait.' "

—TOMMY HENRICH

About this autograph business. Once, someone in Washington sent up a picture to me and I wrote, 'Do good in school.' I look up, this guy is seventy-eight years old.

You done splendid.

I commenced winning pennants as soon as I got here, but I did not commence getting any younger.

(UPI/BETTMANN)

9

With a man that is getting aged, if you rest him every so often you will find that he commences getting limber again with his muscles.

[What Don Larsen was doing when he wrapped his car around a telephone pole at 5 A.M.]
He was either out pretty late or up pretty early.

The only thing Larsen fears is sleep.

[Casey on Don Larsen during 1958 spring training]
Last year he wins five straight before we go into the Series. And I say to him: 'You can win fifty-five straight if you get your arm in shape quicker. Next spring I want you to report ready to pitch.' So what does the feller do? Gets himself married to one of them little airline hostesses, and when he reports I never saw him look so wonderful. I may even pitch him in the opening game. Yes, sir, Eddie Rickenbacker did a great thing when he invented aviation.

I won't trade my left fielder.
[Asked "Who's your left fielder?"]
I don't know, but if it isn't him, I'll keep him anyway.

That fella runs splendid but he needs help at the plate which coming from the country chasing rabbits all winter give him strong legs although he broke one falling out of a tree which shows you can't tell and when a curveball comes he waves at it and if pitchers don't throw curves you have no pitching staff so how is a manager going to know whether to tell boys to fall out of trees and break legs so he can run fast even if he can't hit a curveball?

"*Talk is what mattered to Casey, not drinking. He could drink, but a lot of times he'd have the same drink in his hand for hours.*"

—LEE MacPHAIL

"*On the field he was a teacher, off the field he was a talker.*"

—AL LOPEZ

"Mr. Stengel can talk all day and all night on any kind of track, wet or dry."
—JOHN LARDNER, *Sport*

We don't advocate drinking. But to say that a ballplayer doesn't ever take a drink—regardless of advertisements, some do. Now no ballplayer should ever get into the habit where he drinks before a ballgame. . . . When I had one of those boys, I said, 'Well, this man is limited . . . if he doesn't want to change—why, disappear him.'

[When some young Yankees were playing Twenty Questions after a tough loss]
I'll give you the perfect question for it. Which one of you clowns won't be here tomorrow?

"After suffering through years of [manager Joe] McCarthy's disdain, the sportswriters saw Stengel as a blessing. He always wanted to talk. During spring training he played along with a gag on John Drebinger of the Times, one of the more senior writers. Drebby used a hearing aid. The writers held a special press conference with Stengel, at which the manager mouthed the words instead of saying them. The other writers dutifully took notes. Soon Drebinger was cursing his hearing aid, shaking his head, and saying, 'And I just got new batteries.' It was something that never would have happened in the McCarthy era."
—DAVID HALBERSTAM, *Summer of '49*

I wouldn't admire hitting against [Ryne] *Duren, because if he ever hit you in the head you might be in the past tense.*

[After a reporter asked him if the Yankees had choked in the 1957 World Series]
Ya see, I said 'fuck' to ruin his audio. Then when I started scratching my ass I was ruining his video. He ain't gonna ask me a question like that again.

You gotta lose 'em some time. When you do, lose 'em right.

Most ballgames are lost, not won.

I love signing autographs. I'll sign anything but veal cutlets. My ballpoint pen slips on veal cutlets.

11

Look at Bobby Richardson. He don't drink, he don't smoke, he don't chew, he don't stay out late, and he still don't hit .250.

[After trying the aging centerfielder Joe DiMaggio at first base]
You're gonna make mistakes. You can't worry about them second-guessers.

"We'd have clubhouse meetings that lasted an hour, hour and a half, and if you listened there would be something useful for everyone, but he confused a lot of the players, particularly the younger ones."

—PHIL RIZZUTO

"When I first came up, I was shaving in the locker room. Casey came up and said, 'Kid, I gotta talk to you about a few things.' I stopped shaving and he talked for about half an hour. The shaving cream on my face had disappeared, so I had to start shaving all over. I got to thinking, What in the Sam Hill was he talking about? He was talking about 'these guys' and 'those guys' and 'that lefthander.' It took me almost a year before I could decipher what he was talking about."

—ANDY CAREY

Now you take Ernie Lombardi who's a big man and has a big nose and you take [Billy] *Martin who's a little man and has a bigger nose. How do you figger it?*

"Maybe the reason he rambled when he talked to reporters is he would really be watching the other team practicing. He didn't miss much."

—WHITEY FORD

Going to bed with a woman never hurt a ballplayer. It's staying up all night looking for them that does you in. You gotta learn that if you don't get it by midnight, chances are you ain't gonna get it, and if you do, it ain't worth it.

"I never paid any attention to his doubletalk. No one could duplicate his mind. He'd be sitting on the bench, and you'd think he was asleep. Then he'd flash a sign to [third base coach] Frank Crosetti and things would happen."

—ENOS SLAUGHTER

Good pitching will always stop good hitting and vice-versa.

"*The reason he'd say 'You can look it up' was that he was always rambling back thirty or forty years. And if you did look it up, he was right.*"
—EDDIE LOPAT

"*He talked of nothing but the ballgame, going over and over the plays. This could be in a game we won by 5 to 2. Most managers will analyze a losing game, but Casey is the only one I ever met who took the winning games apart too.*"
—BOB FISHEL

[When a writer told him, "Casey, you haven't answered my question" following a forty-minute lecture]
Don't rush me.

Most people my age [seventy] *are dead at the present time, and you could look it up.*

"*It is erroneous and unjust to conceive of Casey Stengel merely as a clown. He is something else entirely—a competitor who has always had fun competing, a fighter with the gift of laughter. . . . There is wisdom in comedy.*"
—RED SMITH

You're full of shit and I'll tell you why.

"*I remember once he got a letter from a guy in the Army who criticized the way he was handling the ball club. So Casey called in Jackie Farrell, the traveling secretary, and said, 'Do me a favor. Send this guy a telegram. Tell him, "If you're so damned smart, let me see you get out of the Army." ' *"
—YOGI BERRA

[When the Yankees fired him]
I was discharged because there was no question I had to leave.

[In reaction to his firing, which was explained by a club official as part of a youth movement]
I'll never make the mistake of being seventy again.

Casey discussing his firing from the Yankees. Note Howard Cosell in the front row.
(UPI/BETTMANN)

You'd have to say I was fired, because my services were no longer required.

[Final words on his firing]
Don't give up. Tomorrow is just another day, and that's myself. [A year later he was hired by the Mets.]

"Casey had what I call an existential attitude toward life. When bad things happen, you ride with them. When good things happen, don't take them too seriously. He had no illusions. I admire him tremendously for that."

—ROBERT W. CREAMER

WITH THE METS (1962–65)

It's a great honor for me to be joining the Knickerbockers.
[In *Stengel*, Robert Creamer noted that Casey's slip "metamorphosed" the Mets through the basketball Knicks to the baseball Knickerbockers, the team that

(NBL)

15

supposedly played the first formal game under the modern rules in 1845. "Casey had neatly linked the newest team in town with the oldest."]

The Mets are gonna be amazin'.

I may be able to sell tickets with my face.

"One time I was sitting in the bullpen and Casey called up Nelson. Bob Miller got up to start throwing. 'Did you change your name?' I asked him. Turns out Casey referred to Miller as Bob Nelson and [announcer] Lindsay Nelson as Lindsay Miller."

—JOE PIGNATANO

(NBL)

Take those fellows over to the other diamond. I want to see if they can play on the road.

[Asked where the Mets would finish]
We'll finish in Chicago.

[When Tug McGraw told him, "I can get this guy out, I did the last time I faced him"]
Yeah, I know, but it was in the same inning.

[About Frank Thomas, Gus Bell, and Richie Ashburn, who had twenty children among them]
If they can produce on the field as well as off, we'll win the pennant.

[On Shea Stadium]
Lovely, just lovely. The place is lovelier than my team.

This team is strangers with strangers.

[After the team broke a seventeen-game losing streak]
Whew, I thought we would have to call in the fire department, my team's so hot.

"Early in 1962 we're in Philadelphia after finally winning our first game. I'm in the shower and Casey is standing in the middle of the clubhouse. He starts winking at me. Just winking. I can't figure why, so I towel off quickly and come over to him.

"He puts his arm around me. 'You'll love the center-field fence,' he says. 'You'll love the left-field fence.'

"I'm completely baffled. 'What are you talking about?'

" 'Oh! We just traded you to the Cincinnati Reds.' "

—DON ZIMMER

[On Zimmer, who was 0-for-34 at the time of the trade]
He's the perdotious quotient of the qualificatilus. He's the lower intestine.

17

"The best interview I ever had on the air? Well, of course it was Casey Stengel. But I was concerned about him the first time. I knew that Casey talked and talked, and I wondered about getting him off the show. But he quit right at the moment he was supposed to. Then he got up and walked away, and he tore the whole set down. He was still hooked up to the lavaliere."
—RALPH KINER, host of "Kiner's Korner," a postgame television show for the New York Mets

They've shown me ways to lose I never knew existed.

I don't smoke all the time. I stop when I go to sleep.

The way our luck has been lately, our fellows have been getting hurt on their days off.

Ability is the art of getting credit for all the home runs someone else hits.

[In 1964]
Maybe those new people who come out to Shea Stadium and never seen us before will think we're a new team. If they ask me about that other team in those two years I'll tell them they ain't here no more. I fired them for finishing twentieth-tenth each year.

"A laugh a minute. That twenty-three-inning game he used me in the third or fourth inning to pinch-hit. Then in the twenty-third he called me again. I was sitting in the clubhouse dressed in my street clothes. 'Go to the bullpen and get ready to hit,' he said. 'Third game we've played today. You can hit again.' One time Ron Swoboda dove for a ball, hit Roy McMillan ankle-high and tripped him. When Ron got back to the dugout, Casey said, 'That's one of the best blocks I've ever seen in football.'

"The most important thing I can remember him saying was that no matter who's talking, when it goes in one ear and comes out the other, if you would let some of it rub off inside your head it might be useful some day. He was right."
—JESSE GONDER

Players used to sit in the lobbies and talk about baseball. Now they sit in their rooms, watch movies, and forget all about baseball. A lot of them forget about it on the field, too.

"He never called you by name. Just your number. I was 33. The names change, the numbers are always the same."

—RON HUNT

[When he was taking a cab to the ballpark with some writers, the cabbie asked, "Are you fellows players?"]
No. Neither are my players players.

[Pointing to the stands when he removed a pitcher from the game]
Up there people are beginning to talk.

[When the pitcher he was removing told him he wasn't tired]
Well, I'm tired of you.

You say, 'Here is the opportunity' and the Youth of America says, 'How much are you going to pay me.'

Our first Mets game was April 10, 1962. And it was our best game. It was rained out.

The only thing worse than a Mets game is a Mets doubleheader.

Look at that guy. He can't hit, he can't run, and he can't throw. Of course, that's why they gave him to us.

Without losers, where would the winners be?

They gave me a new carpet for my office and the Mets didn't wear that out nor the ballfield.

So now I finally got Harshman [Harkness] *hitting good but I can't fire Canzineri* [Cannizzaro] *and where am I gonna play Charlie Davis* [Smith]*? Everybody wants to buy Big Ben* [Bearnarth] *but who did they give you for him? What about* [Branch] *Rickey? He lives in this town but he won't trade anybody you can make a living with. They say you can't understand me 'cause I talk Stengelese but what about him.*

He talks beautiful but when he's done you can't understand him either.

We woulda beat them if they hadn't commenced being wonderful.

When you're losing, everyone commences to play stupid.

My pitchers done good until they commenced hitting balls over buildings.

(NBL)

"When we were going to face a real good pitcher who threw slow stuff and breaking balls, Casey would say, 'He's gonna give you the Vaseline pot.' "
—MARV THRONEBERRY

[After a long game and an overnight flight]
If any of the writers come looking for me, tell them I'm being embalmed.

Just because your legs is dead don't mean your head is.

"He'd call you 'Doctor' because he couldn't remember your name. Maury Allen, George Vecsey, and I still use the word when we see each other."
—JACK LANG

People don't notice what you're doing bad as long as the effort is there.

Whenever I decided to release a guy, I always had his room searched first for a gun. You couldn't take any chances with some of them birds.

Can't anybody play this here game? [Later transposed in reporting to "Can't anybody here play this game?"]

You couldn't play on my Amazin' Mets without having held some kind of record, like one fella held the world's international all-time record for a pitcher getting hit on the ankles.

"He would talk about game situations from forty years ago, and I was twenty at the time. On a couple of occasions he caught my eye when he was going into those verbal meanders. He would talk in parables. Next thing you know he was talking about a player who was involved in a situation that applied to a situation he had been talking to you about. You realized the story was for you."
—RON SWOBODA

"When he double-talked, he was simply taking pressure off the players."
—ED KRANEPOOL

21

[Advice to Yale-graduate pitcher Ken MacKenzie]
Make like they're the Harvards.

[When MacKenzie said he was the lowest-paid member of the Yale class of 1956]
Yeah, and he's got the highest earned run average, too.

Now there's three things you can do in a baseball game. You can win, or you can lose, or it can rain.

"When we were introduced to the media at a function before our first season, he went around the line-up. He goes to the outfield and starts showing his tremendous

(NBL)

Casey Stengel announces his retirement from Baseball.
(UPI/BETTMANN)

memory: 'Frank Thomas, who had so many homers, Richie Ashburn, a great leadoff hitter and outfielder.' Casey comes to right field—I could see he was having trouble remembering the name—'He hit a lot of homers for Cincinnati, he's a great outfielder.' Casey goes on for a while—'and he'll be ready when they ring the bell—and that's his name, Gus Bell!' ''

—ROGER CRAIG

See that fellow over there? He's twenty years old. In ten years he has a chance to be a star. Now that fellow over there, he's twenty years old, too. In ten years he has a chance to be thirty.

(ROBERT KAUFMAN PHOTO)

Nuts to being old. I'll try to manage as long as I don't have to go to take a pitcher out in a wheelchair.

[Retiring at seventy-five after suffering a broken leg]
I couldn't strut out to the mound to take out a pitcher. It was time to step down.

CASEY FOR THE AGES

I'm a man that's been up and down.

You make your own luck. Some people have bad luck all their lives.

The trick is growing up without growing old.

Just because I'm old doesn't mean I have to be old-fashioned.

I want to thank all the players for giving me the opportunity of being what I was.

Casey celebrating with his players after a win over the Cleveland Indians on August 31, 1950. The win put the Yankees two games ahead in the American League to first place. Left to right are Phil Rizutto, Cliff Mapes, Tommy Byrnes, Joe Page, and Yogi Berra. (UPI/BETTMANN)

I want to thank my parents for letting me play baseball, and I'm thankful I had baseball knuckles and couldn't be a dentist.

Old-timers' weekends and airplane landings are alike. If you can walk away from them, they're successful.

There comes a time in every man's life, and I've had plenty of them.

Sometimes I get a little hard-of-speaking.

CASEY ON THE OP-ED PAGE OF *THE NEW YORK TIMES*

Let me ask you why we can't communicate with those young people and I'll tell you because there's too much fast transportation today if they want to go away from home. The only place you can get anybody to go in is an automobile.

You used to be known in your neighborhood and you had a reputation, and you had the five-cent fare too. Now they want to go someplace where they can get into trouble and they've even got automobiles to get there. So they can go forty miles and disturb people in some other city if they don't want to be seen in their own town. They can even go 300 or 1,000 miles away, and sleep on the ground besides.

The reason is fast transportation, and they've all got automobiles, and there's the airplane, too. There're more places to go to and you can't keep them in anymore, and how can you communicate with them 300 miles away? . . .

But I don't mind the hair, they can wear it any way they want to as long as they don't use fast transportation to get out of their own towns. That's the thing that disappoints me when you ask if I can communciate with them. Not the hair. I wouldn't mind how long they wore it if I could find them and talk to them, and besides they didn't have wigs in those days.

I am trying to be like the Kennedys. I write speeches and I deliver them in a Boston accent. I hold my little finger just *so. I am a bank director. I am going to Europe to deliver one of my speeches and I could make a living by just appearing on televison. I have eighty-nine suits, although I did not used to be such a snappy dresser. I also know a way to make $100,000 quickly, only I am not going to tell anyone else how I do it as they might do it before I could. Right now I remind myself of some of the players I used to manage. I am either out too late or up too early.*

[Asked why the Dodgers were so successful]
You know the owner is smart because he keeps the seats clean. If you wear a clean dress it'll stay clean when you sit down. He runs a public park and he's not going to be arrested for being neat about it. And you know he's kept [manager Walt] *Alston ever since he got him. So that's number two on how you know how smart the owner is.*

Midgets are smart. Smart and slick as eels. You know why? It's because they're not able to do much with those short fingers. You understand? Not being able to do anything with their fingers, what do they do? They develop their brain power.

Baseball is very big at the present time. This makes me think baseball will live longer than Casey Stengel or anybody else.

"Up until his death, Casey loved answering fan mail. Of course, this, too, was done in his fabled eccentric style. When my brother and I wrote to him in the early '70s, all we enclosed for an autograph were two self-addressed postcards. Instead, he used his own envelope and postage, complete with a return mailing label listing his home address in California. His photo (actually a paper baseball with his drawn likeness) was autographed on both front and back. The back was inscribed, 'Good luck Ducks, Tom and Matt' and was signed, 'Casey Stengel, Hall of Famer, N.Y. Mets.' "

—TOM OWENS

"His greatest genius lay in his willingness to adjust to the problems of other men, other times. Despite great age, which is often beset by rigidity of mind, Casey

Stengel remained pliable, understanding, willing to adjust, to change. 'Baseball is changed,' Stengel once said, 'and so is the writing profession.' He knew the newspaper business, understood better than most that the afternoon newspaper reporter could not, as he once put it, 'write the box score.' He got along easily with young reporters. He knew that the world exists on change. He never resisted."

—LEONARD SCHECTER, *The Jocks*

Lefthanders have more enthusiasm for life. They sleep on the wrong side of the bed and their head gets more stagnant on that side.

[On new Busch Memorial Stadium, where the 1966 All-Star Game was played in 113-degree heat on the artificial turf]
Sure holds the heat well.

REPORTER: Would you like to go back to managing?
CASEY STENGEL: Well, to be perfectly truthful and honest and frank about it, I am eighty-five years old, which ain't bad, so to be truthful and honest and frank about it, the thing I'd like to be right now is . . . an astronaut.

IN TRANSLATION

_____ *(A Mere Sampling)* _____

Road apples—Bad players

Clerks—Mediocre players

Sugar plums, green peas—Rookies

Lobs—Batters who can't hit with men on base

Jelly leg—A case of nerves at the plate

He ain't no Ned in the Third Reader, you know—He's been around

Milkshake drinker—A clean-living player

Whiskey slick (a.k.a. whisker slick)—A playboy

He could make a living—A positive assessment of a player

He could squeeze your earbrows off—Description of a particularly tough player

Worm killers—Low balls

Taking it on the big bill—The mistaken practice of outfielders fielding hits on the big, easy hop instead of charging them

2

CASEY ON MANAGING

OR

*"I've Been
Doing Things
That Were
a Little out of the
Way
all My Life
in
Baseball."*

CASEY STENGEL WAS AN ACTIVIST manager in the passive 1950s. Drawing from his main mentor, John McGraw, Casey liked to "manufacture" runs with contact hitting, aggressive baserunning, suicide squeezes, early-game pinch-hitting—and swing for home runs when conditions called for them. Platooning and repositioning his players like the general he was, Stengel was able to win pennant after pennant without overwhelming talent. Part of the reason was that he trusted his coaches and veteran players to teach and lead instead of trying to coach every aspect of the game himself. Another key: Casey took chances by starting younger players when other managers took the safer, no-second-guessing route of using fading oldsters. Stengel even set up a pre-spring instructional school for youngsters that became a major-league model.

As a strategist, Casey was probably best known for popularizing platooning. He usually platooned lefthanded batters against righthanded pitchers and righthanded batters against lefthanded pitchers; this he dubbed "percentage baseball." In 1949 Hank Bauer and Gene Woodling shared right field and together accounted for fifteen homers and ninety-nine runs batted in. But Stengel also violated the percentages, because he remembered who could hit whom and what had happened in past games ("You could look it up"). He was a one-man scouting combine before there were scouts. And a team psychologist before teams hired psychologists.

PSYCHOLOGY

I guess I've been doing things that were a little out of the way for most of my life in baseball. It gave some people the idea that I was just a comedian. When I signed to manage the New York Yankees after the 1948 season, many of the writers couldn't understand why I was brought in to handle such a big job. They had watched some of my work, evidently, as a manager at Brooklyn in the '30s, and at Boston later on. They thought that I wasn't very serious, and that I never cared very much about winning games, and that I was too easy to get along with, and so forth.

But half the time I was too serious, maybe, with my work. When I don't win, I'm good and mad at night. But if you think you're going to do better just by being serious all the time, and never telling any stories or doing any kidding around—why, you're a little mistaken. Some people could never understand that.

The secret of managing a club is to keep the five guys who hate you from the five who are undecided.

"His theory was to play the whole game of baseball relaxed. Maybe that's why he was always cracking jokes: to keep the troops loose."

—JESSE GONDER

"Casey would always tell you to go up to the plate and sing a little tune to relax. So I went up humming one day. Al Lopez was catching for Pittsburgh. 'I guess Casey's been talking to you,' he said. I might have struck out singing."

—SIBBY SISTI

I had this player in Brooklyn and you could ask him for a match and find out what bar he was in the night before. After we traded him to another club I always went up to him before the game with a cigarette and asked for a match. If he pulled out a match from some bar, I knew he had been out late and I could pitch him fastballs.

"**Three** straight no-hitters [by Johnny Vander Meer]? Casey had been coaching at third base, but when the [Boston] Bees came to bat in the fourth inning he switched over to first base. As he crossed the diamond he deliberately passed in front of Vander Meer, who was throwing his warmup pitches, and without turning his head toward the pitcher said quietly, 'John, we're not trying to beat you, we're just trying to get a base hit.' That may have made Vander Meer a little self-conscious; he always remembered Casey speaking to him at that moment. With one out in the fourth inning a Boston batter poked a hit through the middle to end the hitless string."

—ROBERT W. CREAMER, *Stengel*

JOHN MCGRAW AND OTHER EARLY INFLUENCES

"McGraw and Stengel were both very good with young kids. Casey would sit down and talk to them by the hour. He never had any children of his own, so he had a lot to give them. Come to think of it, McGraw had no children of his [own] either. Just thirty years' worth of baseball teams."

—EDDIE LOPAT

[On why he checked breakfast stubs à la McGraw]
You know that the guy who has orange juice, cereal, bacon and eggs, toast and coffee, or an order like that hasn't been up fooling around all night. It's those who order double tomato juice and black coffee who go out to mail letters at three o'clock in the morning.

STENGEL ON MCGRAW

My platoon thinking started with the way McGraw handled me in my last years as a ballplayer on the Giants. [Casey hit .368 when McGraw platooned him in 1922.] He had me in and out of the line-up, and he used me all around the outfield. He put me in when and where he thought I could do the most good. And after I got into managing I platooned whenever I had the chance, long before I came to the Yankees . . .

He wanted you to be a fighter at the plate and not just give in to the pitcher, whatever happened. Stand in there, don't back off an inch, and get a piece of the ball. Something may happen.

He also was very alert on when to start the runners, when to start double steals, and he was very good at not having you caught off a base. He hated to see you just walk off a base sluggishly. He said the first two steps off a base, if the batter hits the ball, might make you be safe at third or safe at home plate.

But after the lively ball came in he knew he had to cut down on the baserunning and go to slugging . . . At the plate he'd let you go for the slug at three and nothing, two and nothing, three and one—if there were men on bases. If there weren't men on bases, he'd get very disturbed at you if you didn't stand up there and fight the pitcher, especially with two strikes.

One day I took a called third strike—the man curved the ball and I was asleep at the plate . . . 'Why weren't you ready up there to fight on that pitch and get a piece of it before it got to the catcher's glove?' And I said, 'Well I thought . . .' and he said, 'Don't think for me. Act.' If you got three or four runs ahead of him at the start of game that would drive him crazy, because then all he could do was try to catch up. He couldn't maneuver as much. . . .

McGraw worked us hard. He'd sit on a chair in front of the boxes behind home plate and watch the entire workout. He wouldn't allow us to stand around the cage between turns at batting practice, the way I'd done on some clubs. You were supposed to bunt the last ball, then run and circle the bases, then go out and practice fielding until your next turn at bat. If he caught you loafing, he'd make a circular motion with his finger, and that meant you had to run and circle the ballpark. A man that came to camp overweight had to run plenty of those laps around the field. . . .

He was strict about everything—probably stricter than any manager could be with ballplayers today. He was the first manager I ever saw who even watched your diet. He went over the players' meal checks in the hotels to see whether they were eating the right kind of meals.

With no night baseball then, he always wanted you in bed by twelve o'clock at night, and he also wanted you out at the ballpark by 10:00 or 10:30 in the morning. . . .

There was no question about any of this with McGraw. If you didn't do it he took some of your money. . . .

Or McGraw would trade you, because he always figured, 'I can buy you back if you're any good.' He didn't carry hatred. If a man had been gone two years, he never said, 'I'd like to get that guy back, but he don't like me and I don't like him.' If the man could help the club win, he got him. Maybe some of my players didn't like me either, but it wasn't because I was that strict. I very seldom fined a man. In my last few years with the Yankees, I didn't have a finger in a single fine that was made on that club. I sometimes threatened players that they were going to run into fines or be traded. But I never did fine a man a tremendous sum. With some of them I could see that it was useless, and anyway, rather than take the man's money during the season, I'd rather give him until the end of the year and then say, 'Well, I can't go to bat with the front office for you on your salary'— assuming that I could do it for some men.

"When [Hughie] McQuillan worked for John J. McGraw and the New York Giants, he shared a room at one time with Casey Stengel, later a manager and a highly respectable character.

" 'I wasn't always so respectable,' says Casey. 'When I roomed with McQuillan I used to wish I could get out at night and play hide-and-seek with McGraw's detectives. But McQuillan kept me honest, because I had to be in the room at midnight to answer his name on the roll call.

" 'McGraw had a system about that time when his chief detective would go around the hotel at midnight, knocking on your door. When he said "Stengel?" I would sing out "Here!" in my baritone voice. Then he would say "McQuillan?" and I would yell "Here!" in my tenor voice. There was never a dull moment.

" 'Since becoming a manager,' adds Mr. Stengel cautiously, 'I have seen the error of those wild ways. If any of my boys stays out all night, I will prob'ly fine their ears off. It's all in the point of view.' "

—JOHN LARDNER, "It Beats Working"

STENGEL ON UNCLE ROBBIE

Every manager I played for on the way up had some outstanding points. . . .

Uncle Robbie [Brooklyn's Wilbert Robinson] was very jolly, and wonderful to work for. He would make you think he thought you were better than you were.

He would take me out of the line-up against the good lefthanded pitchers [Stengel batted lefthanded], but he did it with tact. If he put Jimmy Johnston in there and Johnston didn't get a hit, Robbie would call me over the next day and say, 'Gee, I couldn't sleep last night. I made such a terrible mistake not putting you in that ballgame.' And if it happened another time, he'd say, 'I made that mistake again.'

Now he hadn't made any mistake and he knew it. He just liked to keep you feeling good.

Robbie loved old players—men that were experienced. He loved to get an old pitcher that had a bad arm, because he knew the man was brighter than when he was young and could throw harder. He took Rube Marquard and Larry Cheney and several others that were supposed to be over the hill and made exceptional pitchers out of them, because he showed them how to take advantage of their experience.

And in later years with the Yankees I'd often pick up an old pitcher during the pennant race, like John Sain and Sal Maglie and Jim Konstanty. I'd get the old man to fool the Youth of America. You have the old man go two or three innings in relief, and the young ballplayers can't hit him.

He's too slick for them. He gets them off stride and makes them hit at a bad pitch.

So I followed Robbie's example there. But he hated a little pitcher, which I don't go along with. . . .

The best thing [Pittsburgh's Hugo] Bezdek taught me was that if you have any doubt about how a play should be made, you should find out about it. So Bezdek would hold meetings and ask questions of the experienced players on the club. He'd ask Vic Saier, who had come from the Cubs, how Frank Chance did certain things there. He'd ask Billy Hinchman, a good hitter, what percentages he followed in place-hitting and slugging. He'd ask Max Carey, a great baserunner, what was the best system for running bases. He'd ask his questions about something at a meeting, and then he'd decide, 'This is the way we're going to do it here . . .'

He'd say to a man [Wild Bill Donovan of the Phillies], 'How can you keep making the same mistakes? I was wild when I started out too. But you don't do anything about it. You don't work enough.'

Or he'd say, 'Do you know why I can't keep you in a game nine innings? You've made up your mind in three innings that this just ain't your day. You've got it in your mind that you can only pitch on certain days.'

And I found out as a manager that certain pitchers, with no alibi at all, will get it into their mind that it isn't their day and get off the beam.

You don't copy another manager unless you want to get fired. He was a great man in this town, McGraw, and he won a lot of pennants. But Stengel is in town now, and he's won a lot of pennants, too.

PLATOONING

People said in 1949 what terrible luck we were having, all those injuries, but that was one of the luckiest breaks I ever got, because I had to use the men. If you've got a number of good men setting around on the bench, you'll do yourself a favor playing them, because every time one of my front players got hurt I noticed the fella I stuck in his place would bust out with hits. Then just about the time he slowed down he'd oblige me by stepping in a hole and another fella would step in his place and hit. I decided I'd never count on one player taking care of one position for an entire season. If you've got two or three men who can't play anyplace else, soon you're gonna run out of room for pitchers, and that's why you've got to have players who can do more than one thing.

"Before Stengel, people believed in eight starters, four pitchers, and the bench. Casey actively used players like Hector Lopez. People wouldn't remember his name, but Lopez would be used to spell a Mantle or a Bauer. He'd get a base hit or two—little white rabbits—and then Mantle or Woodling would do the job later in the game. 'This is our part of the game,' they'd say."

—JOHNNY SAIN

I loved to platoon because it upset my players' wives and their parents, who thought they could make more money playing every day and who thought I was crazy. But I told them platooning was a good thing, because on days when their husband or son wasn't playing they could stay home and save the price of a ticket. Also, if you've got some good ballplayers who aren't too strong physically, you can make them into great ballplayers by not playing them every day.

"Casey liked guys who could give you flexibility in times of injury. He had Billy Martin, Jerry Coleman and me, all of whom could play short, second, or third. He had Yogi and Elston Howard catching and playing outfield, and Tom Tresh, who could play short or outfield. All that flexibility helps when you're making out a lineup."

—BOBBY BROWN

We're paying twenty-five men; we might as well let them earn their money.

There's not much of a secret to platooning. You put a righthand hitter against a lefthand pitcher and a lefthand hitter against a righthand pitcher and on cloudy days you use a fastball pitcher.

38

SCOUTING

"Tony Kubek, the shortstop-turned-broadcaster, credits Casey Stengel with inventing the advance scout. Stengel introduced the pioneer in a Baltimore hotel meeting room. The Yankees were going to face Connie Johnson, a black pitcher. Stengel had sent to Baltimore, in advance of the team, Rudy York, the former slugger for the Tigers. York was famous for his ability to read pitchers. 'I'll try,' says Kubek with becoming embarrassment, 'to make it seem not as racist as it was right then. We had only two black players. Elston Howard and Suitcase Simpson, and Mickey [Mantle] and Whitey [Ford] made it all seem funny. Anyway, York says that when Johnson throws his breaking ball, when he goes above his head with his glove, you see a lot of white. "You know how those Negroes"—he used another term—"are. They have those white palms." ' "

—GEORGE F. WILL, *Men at Work*

(UPI/BETTMANN)

COACHING

"Casey never went to the pitching end of it, because he hadn't pitched. He didn't do much about catching, because he hadn't caught and had Yogi and Bill Dickey. Casey mostly talked about outfielding and hitting and running. He didn't know the coaches well when he joined the Yankees; I think he was skeptical about them. Maybe he thought one of them would take his job. But he hadn't been in the American League, and the front office brought them in for him. After the first year, he found what a good staff he had, and he was proud of them. The coaches had a job to do, and he'd tell them, 'They're yours—lock, stock, and barrel.' He was very good about delegating authority."

—EDDIE LOPAT

"Casey would round up a dedicated coaching staff led by Frank Crosetti and Bill Dickey, who drilled the players on fundamentals each year. He felt that everyone should go through fundamentals each spring, because it was easy to forget little things over the winter."

—GIL McDOUGALD

"He had one of the greatest instructional expressions I'd ever heard. He'd talk about a weakness—say, going to your right—and he'd say, 'You've got to eliminate it or learn to protect it or you're not going to be in the big leagues.' Most of the time you'd find out that you couldn't eliminate it. If you were an infielder and you were stronger to your left, you had to play more to the right to protect that weakness. If you were a highball hitter and couldn't hit the lowball, you didn't swing at that lowball until you had two strikes. If you were an outfielder and you couldn't play shallow, you had to play deep. I applied it to every aspect of the game . . ."

—TONY KUBEK

PITCHING

Don't discount that depth. You need it. And if you don't have it when trouble starts, like sore arms and such, you're sunk.

"Other teams had some kid in the bullpen. Casey had someone good to close out the 2–1 games."

—JOHNNY SAIN

What do I care if a starting pitcher finishes or not? We had [reliever] Joe Page, didn't we?

40

"I remember one year when the Yankees had won the pennant, which they always seemed to be doing, and Gil McDougald had had his greatest season. I was in Boston to sign my contract, and a press conference had been set up. I usually took those opportunities to straighten somebody out. One of the writers said, 'Why don't we win more, don't we have a leader?' I said, 'Well, I don't know. I think pitching is important, hitting is important, fielding is important. I think balance on a club is important. What do you mean by "leader"?' He said, 'Well, someone like the Yankees have. Someone like McDougald.' Probably a damn Irish writer out of Boston.

"I said, 'Tell me why you think McDougald's the leader on that club.'

"He said, 'Well, gee, the pitcher gets in trouble. McDougald goes in there and starts talking to him, settling him down. He's important to that club.'

"I said, 'Yeah, you think so, eh? You know the real reason he went in there? Probably because Casey Stengel rubbed an ear lobe or picked his nose to signal for McDougald to get out to that mound and slow that son of a gun down until he could get another pitcher warmed up.' That ended that."

—TED WILLIAMS

FIELDING

"Stengel would often use a hitter near the top of the batting order to give him offensive power early in the game, and then replace him later in the game with a player of superior defensive skills. If he got his lead early enough in the game, he could tighten his defense as early as the seventh inning, instead of remaining vulnerable until the eighth or ninth inning, when his pitching might become tired and easier to hit."

—CLAY FELKER, *Casey's Secret*

INFIELD RULES

"He liked pitchers . . . who could 'throw ground balls,' low pitches that batters tended to hit to infielders who could convert them into double plays. He relished double plays and was always looking for deft second basemen who could 'make the pivot.' He called the double play the most important play in baseball. 'It's two-thirds of an inning!' He'd say, 'One ground ball and [slap of the hands] *two!* You're out of the inning.' For the same reason, he used the sacrifice bunt sparingly, because when you sacrifice you give away an out, and an out is valuable. . . .

'Playing your infield in,' he said, 'turns a .200 hitter into a .300

hitter. . . .' When you have a weak-hitting, righthanded-hitting second baseman batting against a strong righthanded pitcher with a runner on second base, the odds on getting a hit and moving the base runner around to score are not as good as they would be if you sent in a strong lefthanded batter to pinch-hit in the second baseman's place. But if you use the pinch-hitter, how badly do you weaken your defense (hurt your odds) the next inning when you send someone else onto the field in the second baseman's place? To solve that dilemma, Stengel gathered a corps of versatile athletes who could field deftly at different positions, men who were equally at home at second and third, for instance, or at short and second, or at third and short, or sometimes at all three positions. Then if he sent a pinch-hitter in for one man he could put another adroit fielder in his place. Sometimes this involved complexities such as pinch-hitting for the second baseman, moving the incumbent third baseman to second and putting a man from the bench at third, but the defense would remain capable *after* the offense had been improved by the insertion of the pinch-hitters. It worked with other positions, too. Casey might send in a man to bat for an outfielder and then put the pinch-hitter at first base and move the first baseman to the outfield. Or shift a catcher to left field and the left fielder to third base and put a new catcher in who had previously pinch-hit for the third baseman. And so on."

—CREAMER, *Stengel*

HITTING

"Casey had a super memory. If you were a righthanded hitter but couldn't hit off a certain lefthanded pitcher, Casey would remember. He would also remember that a lefthanded hitter had hit well off that pitcher six or seven years ago. That's why he'd make the change. Or when he'd pinch-hit a weaker hitter against a particular pitcher, people would say it was crazy. But Casey knew that this hitter had more success against that pitcher than a stronger hitter. He was amazing that way."

—JESSE GONDER

Percentage isn't just strategy. It's execution. If a situation calls for a bunt and you have a batter who can't bunt, what's the percentage of bunting?

I like good pinch-hitters. I believe that with a lively ball you've got to be an attacker. If I've got a good pinch-hitter, I hate to have him stay on the bench with men on the bases in an early inning. He may end the game right there. He may make them take out their pitcher—a good pitcher that would otherwise have gone nine innings—because he popped him at the right time.

"It was a warm summer evening in the early 1950s, and there was a game at Briggs Stadium (now Tiger Stadium) on a weeknight. The park was filled with a very noisy and excitable crowd, and this particular game turned very early into a slugfest. It was around the fifth or sixth inning, the score was like 8–7 in favor of somebody, and Joe Collins had already hit two home runs. At this point there were two or three men on base, two outs, and it was Collins' turn to bat.

"Joe Collins picked up his bat and started toward the plate. At this instant, Casey called Collins back from the on-deck circle where he had been practicing swinging, and in the next motion called for Bauer or Woodling or someone to get a bat and go up and hit for Collins. Casey was sitting on the steps of the dugout right next to where we were sitting. I then heard the following conversation as Yogi Berra ran over to talk to Casey.

Yogi: 'What's up, Skip?'

Casey: 'I'm batting for Collins.'

Yogi: 'But Skip, don't you know that Joe has already hit two home runs?'

Casey: 'Did you ever see Collins hit three home runs in one game?'

"I'm not sure, but I think the pinch-hitter did indeed get a hit.

"Probably the most interesting thing was that nobody in the dugout said a word or acted in any way as though this were unusual behavior. We thought it was great, and, obviously, have never forgotten it."

—Bert Gordon

CRAIG ON CASEY

"Casey gave me a sense of humor to give to my ballclub. Even as bad a club as we had [with the Mets], Casey had a way of relaxing you, making you feel at ease so you could go out and play your game.

"Before one game I was going over the line-up when I came to the name of Willie McCovey. 'He's a low, outside fastball hitter, so I'm going to play him deep and to pull,' I said. 'Mr. Craig, let me interrupt,' Casey said. 'Where do you want to play your right fielder: in the upper deck or the lower deck?'

"He was concerned about you and your family. 'You pitched out of turn, started and relieved,' he told me one year. 'If you have a problem with your contract, call me.' I got good raises both years I was with the Mets, and he was instrumental. Subconsciously you want to do a little extra for a guy like that.

"He lived in Glendale, California, and he had a listed phone number. He was just another person, not someone hiding behind his celebrity. Casey was good with every person in the organization. The little kid in the clubhouse—he'd made a point of talking to him every day. One of my old coaches, Norm Sherry, told me, 'No matter how bad I feel, I can go in and talk to you. When I walk out, I'll feel better.' That's the same way I felt about Casey. You could talk to him, and he'd make you feel better.

"I think he'd have been able to deal with today's ballplayers making so much money. When the Mets' Kevin McReynolds hit that homer and then signed his big contract for $15 million over four years, I said, ' 'bout time you guys started earning your money.' The players cracked up, but that's what Casey would have said. He would have made a joke of it: It's here and you don't want to run away from it, so you make a joke of it.

"The bottom line is, I'm a better person and a better manager because of the time I spent with Casey Stengel. I only spent two years with him. I wish I could have spent more."

—Roger Craig

EFFECT ON OTHER MANAGERS

"He always called me 'young man.' 'Young man, if you've got two relief pitchers,' he'd say, 'one of them will go bad next year. Get another one.' But that didn't affect my managing. He affected the way I treated people. He was baseball's greatest salesman, because he treated everyone the same. I try to do that, too."

—Sparky Anderson

[Billy Martin's strategy in managing the Twins, Tigers, A's, and Yankees to championships had the stamp of Stengel on it. In fact, Martin was preaching the Stengel line before he ever managed.]

Billy was the most aggressive third-base coach I've ever seen. We must have stolen seven or eight bases that year [1965] because he made a gutsy move with a baserunner. I remember when he first got here, I said to him, 'We've got so much talent here, how come we're not winning?' He told me that we needed to manufacture runs and get guys to be more aggressive.

—SAM MELE

"Billy copied Casey to a T. He used to tell me, 'Watch the old man.' That was what he called Casey. 'Watch how the old man keeps the guys who aren't playing happy.' After a play on the field Casey would turn to them and say, 'What did he do wrong?' or 'You're better than that guy.' Either way, he'd keep them from getting stale."

—MICKEY MANTLE

BILLY ON CASEY

"I was amazed at his loyalty to his players. One time our whole team was involved in a fight on the field, and I turned around, and I couldn't believe it: Casey was right behind me out there ready to go at it if he had to. A couple of times he went out there and got shoved to the ground. . . . He never had a doghouse. If you got in a fight with him, by the next day it was forgotten. And he would talk to me all the time, even when I wasn't playing. He made everyone feel right at home, and when I did play, he was always bragging on me, giving me confidence. . . .

"Casey roomed me with Cookie Lavagetto, who was another extremely intelligent baseball man. Cookie had played ten years with the Pirates and Dodgers. . . . Casey had Cookie work with me. . . . He'd make me sit in a restaurant and stare at a wall without blinking my eyes. I'd practice that for hours. Try it sometime. It isn't easy. He had me do that because he felt that when you were up at the plate, the ball would go by so fast that if you accidentally blinked, that fraction of a second would be enough of a distraction to make you miss the ball. . . .

"He sure knew how to handle players. He'd leave Yogi and Rizzuto alone, because when he got on them, they'd pout and wouldn't play as good as they could, but he could ride Mickey [Mantle] and me, because he knew we responded to that. He was always doing things to me. One day he posted a lineup that had our pitcher, Tommy Byrne, batting eighth and me batting ninth. I blew my top. I took that lineup, and I thumbtacked it

45

to the wall upside down, so now I was batting first. Turned out he was just agitating me, and in the game I batted leadoff, as I did sometimes."
—BILLY MARTIN, *Number 1*

"The biggest thing Casey taught me as a manager was to play baseball according to your personnel. If you had poor pitching and hitting, you had to play for big innings. Casey didn't manage for the crowd. He managed for the players and made the most of their abilities.

"The other thing was how to handle writers. More managers are probably fired by the press than any other way. He knew which ones to get on and which ones to leave alone. I always remember one thing Casey said. 'If a decision goes wrong, never admit it to the press. There's always a reason why you did it.' Be sure to give them the reason. I did and it was helpful."

—RALPH HOUK

"I've always patterned myself after Stengel, Richards, and Durocher, the managers I admire most. They've never hesitated to go out on a limb and take chances that exposed them to second-guessing. . . . Too many managers run their teams to please the fans and sportswriters, an approach that inhibits their decisions. The good manager takes full responsibility for actions that originate with him and says the hell with the consequences. . . .

"When Phil Rizzuto was nearing the end of his brilliant career, Casey consistently lifted him for a pinch-hitter as early as the second inning if he thought a rally was on the fire. Rizzuto probably didn't like it and I know darned well the sportswriters resented such treatment of a longtime favorite, but that didn't stop Casey from making the move. The same goes for his two-platoon system, which ballplayers dislike because it tends to cut down on their salaries. I remember that Casey used seventy-one different line-ups one year, manipulating his men to get the most out of the talent at his command."

—BOBBY BRAGAN

TEACHING YOUNG AND OLD PLAYERS TO MANAGE FOR THEMSELVES

"He was very good at teaching players to think for themselves. He could take both sides of an issue, like a lawyer.

"Casey always spent a lot of time with me. He loved talking to the younger players. That was his way of including them. I was sitting on a train one day and

Casey and Billy Martin after Martin singled in two runs in the bottom of the 11th inning to beat the Athletics and clinch the American League Pennant. (UPI/BETTMANN)

he comes up to me. 'Hey, catcher'—he always called me 'catcher'—'what do you think of the hit-and-run play?' I was just a kid then and I didn't want to disagree with him and we didn't use it much, so I told him I didn't think it was worth a shit. 'You're fulla shit and I'll tell you why,' he begins, and starts telling me how McGraw thought it was a great play, and now he does thirty minutes on McGraw and the Giants and the hit-and-run play. A week later he sees me again. 'Hey, catcher.' Now I'm ready for him. Sure enough, he asks me about the hit-and-run play and I'm smiling and saying what a great play it is and all of a sudden he starts hollering, 'Now wait a minute, for Crissakes, it's a horseshit play and if you listen I'll tell you why.' Damned if he didn't go thirty minutes on why McGraw hated it.''

—RALPH HOUK

"At the All-Star break, Casey would tell the players, 'I know you should be working out for three days, but we're not going to. Take your records with you.' He meant look at the team's record—the Mets were about forty games out—and you know you should be working out.''

—ED KRANEPOOL

"The best thing about Casey was that he'd bring in the old-timers to help the young players. He brought Paul Waner in to play with Brooklyn and Johnny Mize and Enos Slaughter with the Yankees.''

—FRENCHY BORDAGARAY

"Duke Snider [one of the 'old-timers' Stengel brought to the Mets] kind of took me under his wing. He helped me hitting against different clubs. Against some you hit and run, some bunt and run. Any time I came off the field, there was always a place on the bench next to Duke. I wouldn't pout and mope and think about my average: We'd talk baseball. Some of these guys today don't run hard to first. By the time they get there, they have their averages figured out.''

—RON HUNT

"I learned more baseball and had more fun playing one year under Casey with the Mets than in any other season in my entire career.''

—RICHIE ASHBURN

"Nobody knew more baseball or cared more passionately about the game than Casey Stengel.''

—WARREN SPAHN

48

"Casey loved to work with kids. I think that was an asset when he came up to the Yankees, because he had kids who learned how to be good ballplayers. He loved to give the young kids a chance to play."

—AL LOPEZ

"I was playing my first game in center field as a Yankee on a rainy night in Cleveland. I slipped going for a fly ball with the bases loaded and three runs scored. Casey came to me after the game and said, 'Let me see your shoes.' I lifted them up and he saw the spikes were worn down. I was a rookie and I was wearing a pair I had had since high school. He said, 'Young man, go out and buy a pair of shoes and I'll pay for them, but after this you're on your own. This time it's my fault, but if it happens again, it's your fault.'"

—TONY KUBEK

I don't like to talk about a person's age, see? I'd rather talk about his experiences and qualifications, such as either you've got 'em or you don't, and then let age take care of itself. Except in this society, it don't always work this way.

KAVANAGH ON STENGEL

"October 5 [1941] is another of those dates bitterly fixed in tribal Brooklyn memory. Yet it gave me one of my most unique experiences as an Ebbets Field usher. My assignment was the field boxes between the Dodger dugout and the home plate screen. It was fine for collecting autographs, but not tips. Randolph Scott and Groucho Marx led large parties, effusively greeting everyone but ignoring the usher trying to get one last tip with his soon-to-be-retired seat-dusting rag.

"Then Casey Stengel arrived. He was the manager of Boston that season. I remembered him as the Dodgers' manager when I had been a kid getting autographs. His was the hardest to get. Then one day, while the others were chasing someone coming down McKeever Place, I saw Casey walking alone along Sullivan Street. I waited with my back to him, then wheeled around and held out my book. 'Sign for me, Casey, before the others see you.' He did.

"Now I was too mature to ask another grown man to write his name for me. But I was happy with the opportunity the seating arrangements gave me. Apparently his wife, Edna, had found something to do other than come to Ebbets Field. There was an empty seat beside Casey. At a regular season game I might have hustled a fan without a box seat ticket for a couple of bucks to sit there. This time I took it myself.

"Casey accepted me and, with no one else to talk to, the loquacious Stengel carried on a nonstop analysis of the game. He managed for both teams. Like all Brooklyn fans, I had thought I knew everything there was to know about baseball strategy. Casey dazzled me with his anticipation of coming circumstances. He didn't second-guess Leo Durocher or Joe McCarthy, he was two and three innings ahead of the action as he outlined all pending strategy moves.

"It looked good for the Dodgers. They overcame a three-run Yankee lead and went into the ninth inning leading 4 to 3. Hugh Casey retired the first two batters and, as every mournful Dodger fan knows, struck out Tommy Henrich and that should have ended the game. Instead, the ball spun into the dirt and bounced away from catcher Mickey Owen. Henrich ran for first base and the ball rolled all the way to where Casey and I were sitting. It stopped in front of us.

"What followed was a nightmare. The savvy Leo Durocher and his brainy assistants, Chuck Dressen and Red Corridon, let a red-faced Hugh Casey go on uninterruptedly trying to overpower the Yankee batters. As base hits rained all over the park, the Dodgers choked. Owen the catcher, in shock himself for the passed ball, didn't go to the mound to confer with Casey. No one called time. The carnage went on.

"Casey Stengel was nearly out of his mind with frustration as Durocher remained, out of sight, on the bench. At one point, Casey had his leg over the low railing. I thought he was going to go out and stop the action himself. Actually, he was trying to get the attention of the Dodger bench. The side of the dugout blocked him from the view of the players like blinders on a horse. When the Yankees finally were retired, they had a 7 to 4 lead. The Dodgers batted listlessly in the bottom of the ninth. I guess I said goodbye to Casey Stengel as I went off to my postgame assignment. The loss had left me numb. I don't recall leaving Ebbets Field."

—Jack Kavanagh, A *Dodger Boyhood* (Excerpted), *Baseball History 3*

50

(UPI/BETTMANN)

Satchel Paige. (UPI/BETTMANN)

3

CASEY ON PITCHING

OR

"Throw the Ball as far from the Bat and as Close to the Plate as possible."

Modern pitching technique—throwing strikes, keeping the ball down, mixing pitches and locations, using slews of relief pitchers with the crucial "stopper" saved for last—was standard practice for Stengel. But some of his strategy was ahead of any time.

The biggest thing in baseball is a pitching staff. . . .

[On Satchel Paige]
He threw the ball as far from the bat and as close to the plate as possible.

I was a pitcher like Mus-al [Stan Musial] *when I was a slick kid and they had me pitch batting practice. They told me to let them hit it but I wanted to impress everybody so I threw hard. They hit it anyway. I got so damn mad I threw as hard as I could and everything went over buildings. So I told them I was really an outfielder.*

"Casey used to watch the pitcher and see how well he was going. If he had good stuff, we'd leave him in no matter how many pitches he'd thrown. When they count pitches today and take him out after so many, that's the most asinine thing I've ever heard. They forget that the guy's already warmed up and thrown between innings and probably thrown 200 pitches, not counting the game. It doesn't matter. Pitchers like Walter Johnson used to throw every day to keep their arms strong. So Casey would make his judgment on how well the pitcher was going, not how many pitches he'd thrown. He looked for wildness or weakening late in a game."
—AL LOPEZ

"Casey usually left the specifics of pitching up to his pitching coaches, but he had a way of relaxing you when he came to the mound. He could say a negative thing

54

and make it sound positive. I'll never forget one time when he was managing on a cold, crisp day. 'Mr. Craig, what seems to be your problem?'

" *'Well, Casey, those balls seem to be a little slick for some reason.'*

"He kicked the dirt. 'Well, Mr. Craig, you've got about four tons of dirt underneath your feet. Why don't you reach down and rub the ball up?' And he walked off.

"The secret in talking to a pitcher in a crucial situation is not so much what you say as how you say it. You want to say something to relax him so that he can be himself and not show pressure. Casey would never say, 'Don't throw a high curve' and put a negative thought in your head. He'd say, 'Oh, Mr. Craig, you know this guy can't hit a low slider. Why don't you throw one and we'll be out of the inning and in the clubhouse.' "

—Roger Craig

Throw ground balls. . . . Throw those sinkers. Make 'em hit ground balls. Never heard anyone gettin' home runs on ground balls.

"One time Carlton Wiley was pitching against the Braves. We had a one-run lead in the ninth, with two outs and a man on first. I looked over and Casey's foot was on the top step of the dugout. I thought for sure he'd come out and bring in Galen Cisco from the bullpen. But he decided to leave Carlton in. The batter hit a home run to put us down a run, and here Casey comes. He walks out, gets the ball, the pitcher leaves, and here come Cisco. 'Here's the ball,' Casey says. 'There's two outs and nobody on base. I know that for sure.' And he turns around and walks off. When a manager does that, what are you going to do? It keeps you loose.

"Another time Casey was talking at a team meeting in 1963. 'You got a runner on third and you play the infield back. Now, what do us pitchers want to do? Do we want him to hit a ground ball? Of course we don't want him to hit a ground ball, because a run will score. Let's take the chance he'll hit a fly ball. Pitch him high-tight or throw him a change-up.

"Now the infield's in. What do I want him to do? I want him to hit rollies. Ground ball, you throw him out, the run don't score.' "

—Norm Sherry

"He told us always to make sure we stayed ahead of the hitters. 'Those base on balls always hurt you,' he'd say. 'If a guy hits the ball, there are eight men behind you. If you walk him, nobody can help you.' "

—Harry Eisenstadt

*When you pick up a pitching staff, you're getting near the
first division.*

"Stengel decided to pick the runners off third if he couldn't pick them off second.
It depended upon a righthanded hitter being at the plate. The pitcher was to throw
directly at the batter's head, yelling a warning as he let the ball go. The batter hit
the dust, the catcher took the throw on the third-base side of the plate and whipped
the ball to third.

"It was Casey's theory that the baserunner on third would 'freeze' when he
saw the batter hit the ground, and therefore be a stationary target to be picked off.
'I finally had to discard the play,' said Casey [then the Dodgers' manager],
'because the fellows I had playing third for me used to freeze right along with the
baserunner, and our left fielder was kept busy all day running down the ball in the
bull pen.' "

—Tom Meany, *The Saturday Evening Post*

*Mr. Koufax is only the best pitcher in baseball and he fires
as hard in the eighth and ninth innings as he does in the
beginning. Every club has a relief specialist who has made
seven-innings pitchers out of your starters. There aren't
more than seven guys in the league who can give you nine
good innings most of the time.*

CASEY CONTINUES

Why is it the pitchers seldom go nine innings anymore? Some people think
the pitchers used to be in better shape, but I don't think they were. A
pitcher in the wintertime—there generally wasn't any gymnasium for him
to work in. In the summertime they didn't run the pitchers between games
as much as they do now to keep them in shape.

But the old pitcher was throwing the dead ball, and he used to be able
to cheat more. The ball was darker. The infielders would spit tobacco juice
or licorice on it. A new ball would come into the game, and it was passed
around the infield—the man on third would give it a whack, the man on
short would give it a whack, the second baseman would give it a whack.
And when you got it back again you'd say, 'Where's that new ball?' You
had a black ball. That was done with licorice and tobacco juice, and with
black dirt on the infield.

Then some of the old pitchers threw the spitball, and some would throw the shine ball, where they'd keep paraffin alongside their trouser leg and shine one side of the ball with it to make it break sharper. If the ball had a tear in it in just one spot, that was what the pitcher wanted.

Today the balls are slicker. They use seventy balls in a game. The umpires examine the ball all the time, and if there's a scuff mark on it, they throw it out. They try to keep you from throwing spitters, or doing anything to make it easier to sink the ball.

The old pitchers who went the nine innings learned to pace themselves. They could stand out there and use that arm and use rhythm—a curveball and a fastball and a change-up. Those were the three main pitches they had in those days. They pitched half with their arm and half with their head.

Nowadays you can't wait on the pitcher to pace himself. That lively ball with the cork center and the yarn wrapped tighter—there's so much slugging that the pitcher has to bear down all the time.

Why strain a starting pitcher by keeping him in there when you're going to need him over a long pennant race?

I'd rather not wait too long to take a pitcher out. I will often take him out if the other team hit the ball hard the inning before, even if the balls were caught—unless it's a case where he has an eight- or ten-run lead and he's just tossing the ball up there and letting them hit it, to save his arm for the late innings.

But if I see in the sixth inning, say, that he's pumping and throwing his hardest and yet they're still hitting him, I'll put another man in the next inning, because I figure he'll go worse from then on. And when the second pitcher goes in there, I'll have a third one warming up. So if my second pitcher walks the first two hitters or something like that, then I'll have a third shot at stopping the other team.

"Different pitchers grip the ball different ways. I used to hold the ball across the seams, using all four of them. I felt it gave my ball a rise and a good break on the curve. I was kind of a dart thrower. I didn't have a long, loose motion like Raschi's. I did pick up a slider with the Yankees. I tried to pick up a change-up like Lopat's, but I didn't have quite the motion—too short.

"Lopat almost never threw the ball in the strike zone. He told me one of the tricks of the trade was to make batters go after bad pitches—part of Casey's philosophy as well. Casey talked about not losing your temper. Sometimes, if you've

given up a few hits or walks, you rear back and throw the ball down Broadway. Casey said, 'That's when the batter makes the ball disappear on you.'

"Casey had confidence in using me with men on base, even when I couldn't get the win. Just for half an inning or an inning. I was coming in so often with men on base that I thought I had two infields."

—ALLIE REYNOLDS

LOPAT ON TECHNIQUE

"Pitching technique depends on the individual. Some hold the ball with the seams, and the ball don't do nothing. So you let them hold it across the seams. Power pitchers mostly do. The upspin you get makes the ball carry about chest-high. Koufax, Virgil Trucks, Dizzy Trout—they all pitched over the top and had power. The average pitcher throws across the seams and it goes straight. So you give it to them with the seams and it sinks. That's what you're looking for: movement. You experiment with these guys, especially the young fellows. You sometimes have to sacrifice velocity for movement. No matter how hard you throw, you're not going to throw it by them in the seventh, eighth, and ninth because you've lost a little power.

"Before I came over to the Yankees, Ted Lyons polished me off with the White Sox. He taught me to short-arm and long-arm my pitches. You have the same motion, but one time you extend your arm all the way while throwing, and another you just snap it through. Those two deliveries and throwing from different angles—overhead, sidearm, and three-quarters— create different pitches. So you're throwing ten, twelve, fourteen pitches if you break it down.

"Power pitchers rarely have change-ups. They're reluctant to do it. Koufax was one who could. Other power pitchers don't develop one until their careers get into the twilight zone. Koufax put it together when he put together the other stuff.

"You had to get it into the strike zone to get ahead of the hitters. You learn the characteristics of the hitters. A Williams or a DiMaggio will set on a pitch that you got him out with on the previous at bat. That's the Ph.D of pitching—when you can watch the hitter and tell from his reflexes what kind of pitch he's looking for. Let's say I get Ted Williams on a fastball the first time up and then a curve. The next time up—it may be the sixth or seventh inning—I deliberately throw the ball two feet outside. He doesn't swing for it, but he's starting to take an uppercut as if he were. You can tell what he was looking for based on his reflexes. Was he a little late on it or was he out in front? But your analysis better be right.

"Say he showed me he was late. [He was looking for a curve.] The next pitch would be a fastball, but in on him. That way, if he hits the fastball, it'll go foul. Then I'll come back with something else, but in a different spot. My theory with Ted was, never in the same spot twice. He told me later on, 'I could never figure you out.'

"When I was with the White Sox I got him out four times with a screwball and a change-up. A month later I was pitching against him in Yankee Stadium and I got him out the first two times on fastballs and sliders. The first time I got two strikes on him and didn't show the change-up. Then I gave him the screwball and he hit it down to short and we threw him out at first. I did it the second time up *after* two strikes.

"The hitters will look for certain pitches up to two strikes. But with two strikes they can't afford to look for the same pitch anymore. Some hitters, though, would gamble. Like Gene Woodling. He'd give you a time at bat, but he'd get that pitch, you see. He'd go down the line with you looking for a pitch. If you gave him something else with two strikes, he'd take it and strike out. But the next time up he'd be ready for the pitch and if you threw it to him he'd kill you.

"I don't think Casey knew what I was throwing half the time. The method of operation was relayed to him by [pitching coach] Jim Turner. On the field, though, there was discussion. In the 1953 Series against the Dodgers I had them beat 4–2 in the top of the ninth. I got the first guy out. The next guy singled. Then I got the next guy out and I walked the next guy. So we got two men out and two on. Duke Snider was the hitter. Casey came rambling out of the dugout and called Yogi over. 'How ya feeling?' he asked me. I said, 'Feelin' fine.' And he said, 'You sure?' He turned to Yogi: 'What about it, Yogs?' 'Yeah, he's all right.' Casey turns back to me: 'You ain't lyin' to me, are you?' I said, 'How long have I been pitching for you?' 'Six or seven years.' 'Have I ever lied to you?' 'No.' 'You think I'm going to start now?' And he turned around and left. I got Duke Snider to ground out to second base for the final out of the ballgame.

"We had to give credit to Casey because he listened to Turner. A lot of managers won't listen to the pitching coach. There were times when Casey could have panicked and started using us more than we had been, but Turner kept him from it.

"I was the pitching coach in 1960. We'd go over the hitters, and I'd say, 'Who do you want in the third inning?' He was liable to pinch-hit for a guy in the second inning and have no one warmed up. He never thought about that. He said to me about the pitchers, 'They're yours, lock, stock, and barrel.'

"But we had a problem with Ralph Terry. I had to fight like hell to get him into the line-up. He was sort of an experimenter. Casey would call him Thomas Edison. 'Young man,' he'd say, 'if you don't like it here, we can send you where you came from.' He was from Kansas City, and that was a real no-no. At one time Terry had seven pitches. He blew a 6–1 lead in Kansas City by throwing some sliders. I told him, 'Forget your slider, work on your curve and bring up your change and fastball.'

"Terry was in the doghouse for a while. I told Casey, 'We can't afford anyone in the doghouse. We either use him or we don't use him and get rid of him.' He said, 'We'll see, we'll see.' I kept working on him. Finally, we got a spot. We got into the seventh inning in Boston. I said, 'We got Ralph Terry.' 'No, no,' said Casey. 'We don't have anyone else,' I said. Casey brings him in with men on first and second and out one, and we're leading by one. Terry gets the side out in the seventh, the eighth, and the ninth, and we win 2–1. 'Now,' I told Terry, 'you're giving me some ammunition to work with.'

"But every time I bring up Terry's name, Casey says, 'No, no.' 'Case, the guy's given us two and two-thirds innings, don't we gotta keep using him?' We go to Cleveland and I tell Ralph to be ready. Sure enough, Casey brings him in in the sixth inning after asking me, 'You got him ready?' And Terry protects a one-run lead for the last four innings.

"I go to Casey the next day. We had some doubleheaders coming up so I thought it would be easy. Casey was still reluctant, but I finally convinced him. Terry started and won and got back on track again."

—EDDIE LOPAT

"If he wanted to knock somebody down, he'd knock himself on his chest to signal, 'Plug him.' He did it so hard he would just about knock himself down."

—ED KRANEPOOL

"The main thing is not to mess up your pitching staff. A lot of guys use a pitcher one day, the next, and the next until he runs out of gas. Casey let Jim Turner run things, more or less, because Turner had been a pitcher and Casey hadn't. I more or less let Harry Brecheen run the pitching. Both Casey and I kept a book *of what pitchers did every day, and we went more or less according to that. When we [Baltimore Orioles] won the pennant in 1966, the only guy who pitched every day was Stu Miller [a junkball pitcher]; he couldn't hurt his arm the way he pitched."*

—HANK BAUER

"The man who throws the ball gets the credit. I'll take the money. I was the pitching coach, not the manager. Casey gave me carte blanche *with the pitchers. I'd always take my list in there—so-and-so's pitching tomorrow, we've got so-and-so in the bullpen, number one and number two—and Casey never changed it one time in eleven years. He trusted me, and I had great respect for him because of that. We never had one cross word in eleven years.*

"If it was the last game of a series, we'd discuss the next series. I'd say, 'I've got Reynolds and then Lopat and then maybe Ford or Raschi.' Reynolds, Raschi, and Lopat—I'd give them the greatest credit in the world. They won 270 games in five years. I'd try to set them up three, four, five days ahead.

"We might discuss when to take a guy out, but it was Casey's decision when he gets in trouble from the seventh on. I never went out to take a pitcher out. My job was to know everything there is to know about a pitcher. A pitching coach should know every thought a pitcher has—he should be that close to him.

"All Casey and I discussed was a player and his health, not the fine parts of pitching. I never heard him bawl a pitcher out. He'd never low-brow you and say you shouldn't have done this. He wasn't a second-guesser. He made his own decisions, and that was it."

—JIM TURNER

"I used to work closely with Watty Clark, a good lefthanded pitcher, and I learned a lot from him. The key to throwing to first is not going with the same routine all the time. Wait another second before you throw, less the next time. If you have a set routine, the great baserunners will pick it up. 'A few times throw over there and give him a lousy move so he thinks it's your good move,' Watty would say. Casey knew this and approved of it.

"The major thing in setting up a hitter is knowing his strengths—is he a lowball hitter or a highball hitter? In meetings before the games the pitcher would say how he was going to pitch a hitter. The only guy Casey didn't pay too much attention to was Van Lingle Mungo. He could throw the ball by you, so he got batters out throwing to their strength. Casey would say to the fielders in meetings with Mungo, 'Well, be alert' or 'Be alive.' Once I threw outside when I should have thrown inside, and the guy hit a line drive to the outfield. I was lucky it was caught. 'Well,

you can make one or two mistakes,' Casey said. 'We can't throw the ball where we want to all the time.' He knew when to get on your ass and when to give you a pat on the back."

—HARRY EISENSTADT

[On Mets' Larry Bearnarth]
He is an inexperienced pitcher, but he gets out of that hole. Big uniforms and big names don't frighten him. He throws those double-play sinkers to them all.

"He didn't believe in highball pitchers. 'You gotta have lightning to pitch high,' he told me, 'and you don't.' "

—LARRY BEARNARTH

[On Johnny]
Sain don't say much, but that don't matter much, because when you're out there on the mound, you got nobody to talk to.

[To Tracy Stallard of the 1963 Mets]
At the end of this season, they're gonna tear this joint [the Polo Grounds] *down. They way you're pitchin', the right-field section will be gone already.*

[On Eddie Lopat, who looked to Stengel as if he were "throwing wads of tissue paper"]
Every time he wins a game, people come down out of the stands asking for contracts.

[After Lopat faced a fellow junkballer, Brooklyn's Preacher Roe, in Game Three of the 1952 World Series]
You pay all that money to great big fellas with a lot of muscles who go up there and start swinging. And those two give 'em a little of this and a little of that and swindle 'em.
[The Dodgers won 4–3.]

[Why he started Eddie Lopat in Game Seven]
There were fifty-five reasons why I shouldn't have pitched him, but fifty-six reasons why I should. [Lopat and three other Yankee pitchers beat the Dodgers 4–2.]

"Casey believed you shouldn't give a batter a pitch he could hit: If you're a sinkerballer and the guy likes a low pitch, throw him outside. Casey felt if you couldn't go to the corners, you couldn't win.

He believed in getting ahead of the hitter. Get a pitch he doesn't expect over the plate right away—a curve, say, to a fastball hitter. Casey never wanted to give in, though. He felt it was better to go to 3-and-2 than go down the middle on 2-and-2."

—SOLLY HEMUS

"I used to hit his pitchers pretty good, so they'd often throw at me, which got me mad—I'd go crazy—and it made me more aggressive at the plate and on the basepaths, so he'd shout to them, 'Don't wake him up!' He also knew that I was a bad-ball hitter, so he'd tell his pitchers, 'Just throw him strikes!' I remember a game in the late fifties. I was at bat. There were dark shadows in the seventh inning, and Casey brought in Ryne Duren, who wore dark sunglasses and was an alcoholic. He threw the first warm-up pitch into the stands and my legs started shaking. After some more wild throws, I nervously got ready for my first official pitch. But Duren started squinting, trying to make out Yogi's sign. Then he took off his glasses and cleaned them off. My anxiety increased. Finally, he threw a fastball behind my back. I got off the ground and took my bat and walked over to the Yankee bench, where everyone was laughing. I told Casey, 'Listen, old man, if he hits me, I'm not going to fight him, I'm going to fight you!' Of course, I didn't want to fight him. I was just so nervous I had to say something. Casey just kept laughing."

—VIC POWER

[On Warren Spahn, then a Boston Braves pitcher, whom Casey had farmed out for supposedly refusing orders to hit a batter]
I said 'no guts' to a kid who wound up being a war hero and one of the best pitchers anybody ever saw. You can't say I don't miss 'em when I miss 'em.

Casey always had his best pitchers start. There was no such thing as middle relief. Just four or five starters and Joe Page. He let Turner run the staff. If Casey came out to the mound, it was to take you out. The only time I got mad at him was when he didn't start me in the first game of the 1960 World Series. He started Art Ditmar. Casey never said a word, and I never knew the reason."

—WHITEY FORD

Casey thought Ford's arm was tired and needed an extra day's rest. Ditmar lasted one-third of an inning and lost 6–4. Ford pitched shutouts in the third and sixth game. He wasn't fresh enough to start the Series-deciding seventh game, and the Pirates won 10–9. Casey later told his business manager Bob Case that his greatest regret was not using Ford to relieve in Game Seven.

STENGEL ON PITCHING TO HORNSBY

On the Philadelphia [Phillies] club at that time we had Lee Meadows, a very good pitcher who wore glasses. He was our Saturday pitcher—with no Sunday baseball in Pennsylvania then, that was when they drew the biggest crowds.

One day with Meadows pitching we were playing St. Louis. Branch Rickey was their manager. They had men on second and third with two out in the ninth and Rogers Hornsby, the greatest righthand hitter in the National League, at bat. Our manager ordered Meadows to give Hornsby an intentional walk—he put up four fingers so that everybody could see. I was out in right field, and I was hoping Meadows would walk Hornsby, because that was what I thought the situation called for.

But Meadows reared back and threw the first pitch over for a strike. So Hornsby leveled off for the next pitch, and Meadows threw a fastball behind his head. That was one and one. Then Meadows broke a curveball over the plate for strike two.

After that he threw ball two behind Hornsby's head, and ball three behind his head. Now Meadows thought he could get Hornsby on a curve-ball for the third strike, but Hornsby stepped into it and hit the darnedest line drive I ever saw. It went out there just about three feet off the ground, but it carried all the way to the left fielder, and he caught it to end the game.

As Meadows went into the clubhouse he had to pass Branch Rickey, and Rickey said, 'Young man, you'll pay for that some day.'

Anyhow, that was the roughest I ever saw a man pitched to in the major leagues. But the biggest thing was what Hornsby did, after having all those fastballs thrown behind his head. Instead of falling away from the plate on that last curveball, he stepped in and hit a tremendous line drive.

"The number one thing he taught me about pitching was to pitch my own game rather than the hitter's. That meant having good control, getting ahead of the hitters and staying ahead of them, and using few pitches."
—ALVIN JACKSON

"You can only throw so many balls as a pitcher. Casey had us doing shadow work. We'd stand on the mound, keeping runners on or preventing suicide squeezes with fake kicks and throws. That was especially useful the spring of the 1990 lockout."
—LARRY BEARNARTH

"One day Casey goes out to the mound to remove Bobby Shantz. He had Johnny Kucks, a sinkerballer, all warmed up in the bullpen. Casey comes limping back to the dugout, arguing with [pitching coach] Jim Turner about something or other. The first guy pops up, and the second guy hits into a double play. Casey missed it all, arguing and yelling with Turner. He never realized that he had mistakenly called for Virgil Trucks when he meant Johnny Kucks."
—RYNE DUREN

[On August 20, 1963, a twenty-two-year-old rookie lefthander named Grover Powell threw a four-hit shutout to beat the Phillies and become the Mets' first overnight sensation. Afterwards, pad and pencil in hand, Casey joined the crowd of newspapermen crowded around Powell and asked the most provocative question.]
Wuz you born in Poland?

[Also on Powell]
Not bad for a fourteen-year-old pitcher. Just imagine what he'll be like when he's sixteen. [In Powell's next start Pittsburgh's Donn Clendenon hit a line drive off his cheek, and he never won again.]

"One spring Mark Freeman, an educated man, was on the verge of making the pitching staff when he broke his windup and balked the winning run home in an exhibition game. Stengel was talking to his writers the next day when Freeman decided to put him on the spot: 'Casey, I got to ask you, what do you do with the bases loaded, Al Kaline at bat and a bug flies in your eye?'
"Stengel paused for the attention of all the players and writers and replied: 'Son, you got to learn to catch those bugs in your mouth.' "
—STEVE JACOBSON, *Newsday*, August 26, 1990

65

[Seeing old Satchel Paige warm up for the St. Louis Browns]
Get the runs now! Father Time is coming!

CASEY ON THE SPITBALL

I have seen a lot of stuff about the spitter, how it was barred in 1920 on account of it was in the same class with the shine, emery, talcum, tobacco juice and phonograph needle balls which produced a grand carnival of cheating.

Now, they were right to bar all them cheating deliveries. But the spitter wasn't anything like all the other pitches. Sure, it meant using an outside agency. But developing the spitter meant honest effort. The umpire saw what the pitcher was doing out in broad daylight. There were no night games.

Well, the spitter and the cheaters were making the pitchers too strong. So the club owners, which they were after more hitting, barred the spitball along with the other 'foreign agency' deliveries, and gave the spitter a bad name.

Another thing worked against the spitter. We began to get more women at ball games and some of the owners became fancy, thinking of sanitation.

They said the spitter was filthy. Well, it wasn't any Little Lord Fauntleroy pitch. Some of the hurlers really slobbered all over the leather. But it deserved a better fate and a better name.

4

CASEY ON FIELDING

OR

"You Gotta Get 27 Outs to Win."

68

EVER SINCE BABE RUTH and the clean, spitless ball joined forces in 1920, fielding has been the poor stepchild of baseball. By the time Stengel took over the Yankees in 1949, managers were waiting numbly for home runs and complete games to do the work for them. Stengel liked sluggers as much as anyone, but not if they couldn't field. He realized that the best pitching in the world would be worthless if it wasn't backed up with superior fielding. And he knew the surest way to field a good team when injuries hit was to have fielders who could handle more than one position.

I don't like them fellas who drive in two runs and let in three.

[Asked about the prevalence of one-handed fielding]
I would have to say that maybe they are okay today, but that years ago we couldn't make them because of the size of our gloves, which were much too small to be worn on a hand. But I do not like to see people use just one part of their body, which is what they do when they catch a baseball with one hand. A man should be able to throw with both hands and run with both legs. But kids grow so fast today that I catch myself looking at too many one-legged players and that ain't right. Anyway, if you caught a baseball one-handed in my day, you were known as a showboat and the manager would fine you.

A double play gives you two twenty-sevenths of a ballgame.

Some managers have one special way they want double plays to be made. My system was, make it any way you can. But be sure to find some way to make it, or I can't play you.

69

"Casey believed in quick feet and hands, but mainly quick feet. He used to say, 'Your feet will make your hands quick.' We always took eight to ten rounds of infield practice before every game to loosen up. Casey said, 'If you're too hurt for infield, you don't play.' "

—TONY KUBEK

Even with the better equipment and the better grounds, you have to have more ability to be an infielder or an outfielder today, because the lively ball comes at you quicker. You have to start faster because of the speed of the ball. It goes through the infield faster. And if you're an outfielder—in my day we could run and overtake the ball if the park was large enough. Now you can't get to it half the time. You can't overtake it unless you're a Mantle or a DiMaggio or one or two other amazing men that get such a start it's noticeable that they're really catching up with that ball.
And that's why I say that the outfielders of today are greater. And the infielders are greater.

Now to be prepared is to have a lot of players for each position. You've got to have fellows who can move around. It's obvious if at each position you got two or three guys who can't play anywhere else you're gonna soon run outta room for pitchers, so that is why you've gotta have players who can do more than one thing.

"Casey gave guys a financial incentive for playing several different positions. The big prize used to be the extra money you'd get at the end of the season for making the World Series. If you could play extra positions, you'd help your team get there. You'd also get recognition: Even a utility player like John Blanchard had a Camel ad you'd see in the subway. Nowadays the postseason money isn't that enticing; you make your big money not so much by being versatile as by specializing in one position."

—ROD KANEHL

[Watching outfielder Norm Siebern joke around the batting cage the day after Siebern lost several balls in the sun in a 1958 World Series game]
A man drops two or three fly balls in the sun, you'd think he'd get a glove and go out there and practice a little.

70

[Yankee infielder] Bobby Brown reminds me of a fellow who's been hitting for twelve years and fielding one.

When a fielder gets the pitcher into trouble, the pitcher has to pitch himself out of a slump he isn't in.

CASEY ON FIELDING PITCHERS

I bet I lost six games fieldin' by a pitcher. He's got an $18 glove, ain't he? He ain't blind. He's got good eyes, but he's a pitcher. Fieldin' ain't his job. So I lost six games fieldin' by a pitcher.

"He'd always talk to you as a third party. He'd walk up and down the dugout talking, but you knew exactly who he was talking about. One time there were runners on first and second in a bunt situation. People are always taught to bunt toward the third baseman on this play. 'If I was a lefthanded pitcher,' Casey said, and I was the only lefthanded pitcher on the bench so I knew who he was addressing, 'I'd take a little off a slider and go to the third-base line.' I listened to him, and in eight years I never let a man get bunted to third."

—ALVIN JACKSON

[On Bobby Shantz]
I've been around this game for fifty years, and that boy is the best fielding pitcher I ever saw. [Unfortunately, Stengel removed Shantz at an inopportune time of the 1960 Series finale. Shantz's replacement, Jim Coates, failed to cover first quickly enough and opened up a big Pirate inning. The Yankees eventually lost 10–9, and some Yankee fans never forgave Stengel for making the change.]

CASEY ON CATCHING

[On why the Mets used their first draft choice to take veteran Hobie Landrith]
You have to have a catcher, because if you don't, you're likely to have a lot of passed balls.

[On Mets catchers somewhat later]
I got one that can throw but can't catch, and one that can

catch but can't throw, and one who can hit but can't do either.

[After the Mets' Chris Cannizzaro made two errors in a game]
He's a remarkable catcher, that Canzeroni. He's the only defensive catcher in baseball who can't catch.

"Chuck Klein beat the Dodgers out of a tough ball game in Philadelphia, hitting a home run off [Dutch] Leonard with a couple on in the ninth.
  " 'What kind of a pitch did Klein hit?' Stengel asked his catcher.
  " 'Fast ball,' grunted [Babe] Phelps.
  " 'Why didn't you call for the knuckler?' demanded Stengel.
  " 'Why should I?' Phelps wanted to know.
  " 'Why should you!' screamed Casey. 'It seems to me if you have so much difficulty catching it, the guy might have had at least a little difficulty hitting it.' "
  —TOM MEANY, *Saturday Evening Post*

[In 1966]
The Mets have always had trouble at catching. Not the Yankees, though. After Bill Dickey they had Mr. Berra who swung that bat pretty good and Elston Howard gave me many excellent years.

[Frank] *Bruggy was catching, and* [Phillies manager Wild Bill] *Donovan kept yelling to him from the bench, 'Mix 'em up! Mix 'em up!' So Bruggy called for every different pitch he could think of, and still the Athletics kept hitting them safe. And Donovan kept yelling, 'Mix 'em up!' Finally, Bruggy called time. He turned so Donovan could hear him, and he yelled to the pitcher, 'If you have anything else in your repertoire, please deliver it!'*

"At one camp Casey brought in Bill Dickey, Mickey Cochrane, and Gabby Hartnett to talk to the catchers. Dickey did most of the instructing. They told us to be lightfooted, quick with our legs on the steal. It was important to have your weight underneath you, because if you're off-balance, you'll bounce the ball ten feet short on the throw. When you're catching, you should put your right thumb under your index finger and make a soft fist to keep it there. You learned never to throw a change-up to a Punch-and-Judy hitter like Nellie Fox. You have to go after the bandies, the rooster hitters: Pour the coal to them. We were also told to wear cups—many moms and dads forget.

"Dickey was especially helpful to me. In the spring of 1959 he asked Casey if he could teach me to catch. I'd been an outfielder, but I made the club as third catcher.

"We catchers were always talking among ourselves. If the Red Sox were coming to town, we'd find out who the hot hitters were. Yogi would say, 'You gotta jam this guy.' Ellie [Howard] would say, 'You can set him up with a fastball and get him out with a curve.' "

—JOHN BLANCHARD

"When we played the Pirates in the 1960 World Series, he switched Berra and me, moving Yogi to the outfield where I usually played and putting me behind the plate. The fans thought Casey was just being cute. But he knew the Pirates had some fast runners, and because my throwing arm was stronger at the time than Yogi's, he reasoned that I was better equipped to keep Pittsburgh's baserunners 'honest.' "

—ELSTON HOWARD [In the seven-game series Howard was the starting catcher four times. Pittsburgh had two stolen bases, both off Berra.]

[Describing for *Life* magazine how Dodger catcher John Roseboro prevented the White Sox from stealing bases in the 1959 World Series]
Roseboro took the go-go-go out of the White Sox and changed it to stop-stop-stop. Now this is an outstanding thing because it hurt their style of play and what's more disrupted their spirit.

"I learned about catching from Jim Hegan when I was with the Yankees [1961–62]. He taught me not to try to get in front of everything. That had been the old way of doing things. But if a wild fastball pitcher like Ryne Duren was pitching, Hegan told me, you don't have time to get over there to catch an outside pitch.

"Hegan told me to receive the strikes and catch everything else. By 'receive,' he meant to look good. Don't block the umpire and look as smooth as possible. Anything that's obviously not a strike, catch it any way you can—especially with men on base. There was no such thing as looking pretty with those pitches. That was just a theory. Just catch the ball or block it. The way you look won't have any bearing on its being called a strike."

—JESSE GONDER

73

"One of the most important things is to gain the confidence of the pitcher. When you have the confidence of each other, like a jockey and his horse, you'll do well. It also helps to know his nature: what his best pitch is, what his second best pitch is. Yogi was an astute student of pitchers. Being the great hitter that he was, he gave them great confidence in his judgment of other hitters and how to pitch to them. His greatest attribute was knowing what hitters could hit and in what situations to call certain pitches."
—RALPH HOUK, on the qualities that he and Stengel appreciated in Berra

"If a catcher has his pitchers' confidence, they'll know he's not a dummy back there. They won't have to worry about whether he's calling the right pitch. When I left Brooklyn, Babe Phelps became the catcher. Van Lingle Mungo had been a great believer in me. He had a hell of a time with Phelps because he didn't believe in him. Van was already a wild man; now he had something else to gripe about."
—AL LOPEZ [After five consecutive winning seasons with Lopez, Mungo had four consecutive losing seasons with his successors.]

"One of the most serious injuries occurred on August 7 when Yogi Berra was hit on the left thumb during a game against St. Louis, and the thumb was fractured. With the Red Sox coming on, the most important of their young power hitters was sidelined—a real blow. Nor was Berra a quick healer. Finally, on August 25, Dr. Sydney Gaynor, the team doctor, visited him and said that the cast was ready to come off and he could play. But just when Stengel was ready to play him, the Yankees went to St. Louis, and Yogi visited with his family. His mother took one look at the thumb, cut open a lemon and placed it on the thumb, and told him not to take it off for a certain number of days. This was the way injuries had been healed in her family in the past, and this was the way they would be healed now. When Berra joined the team later in the day, the lemon was still there. Stengel wanted to put him back in the lineup immediately. Berra refused. He was not playing until the allotted number of days had passed and it was time to take off the lemon. Folk medicine triumphed over modern medicine. He followed his mother's instructions, not those of Sydney Gaynor. 'My catcher, Mr. Berra,' Stengel told the writers, 'is wearing a lemon instead of a mitt.'"
—DAVID HALBERSTAM, *Summer of '49*

"Casey always used to emphasize the positive. He'd say, 'If you're not hitting, try to outdo the other catcher behind the plate . . .'

"He let me call my own games. I studied the hitters a lot. I really did, and he knew that. He just said, 'Keep it up, kid.'

"I would tell him when a pitcher was starting to lose it by wiggling my fingers behind the plate. It was a signal to him to get somebody up in the bullpen.

"I could tell when Whitey was getting tired when he started to drop his arm down a little on his release. Same with Raschi and Reynolds."

—YOGI BERRA

CASEY ON FIRST BASE

They protect you in the field . . . with the appliances. *They give them* appliances *that are like a net. The first baseman used to carry a postage stamp, now they carry fishing nets.*
They used to say, 'Two hands for the beginners,' but it counts just as much if he catches it with one hand, don't it?

Yogi Berra. (AP/WIDE WORLD PHOTOS)

"I started as a shortstop and moved to third base. Andy Carey, Bill Johnson, Bobby Brown, and Gil McDougald were there, so I tried outfield. I was almost hit in the head out there. 'Moose, the only way to the big leagues for you is first base,' Casey told me. In spring training he sent me to the Arthur Murray dance studio in St. Petersburg three nights a week to learn to shift my legs. I liked to dance anyway. I did the polka and Polish hop.

"Casey kept after me. When I made an error hitting a runner on the 3-6-3 double play, he said, 'Moose, did anyone ever tell you how to throw?' He had Frank Crosetti teach me to throw to the infield side of second when I was holding the runner, and to the outfield side when I was playing behind him.

"If I made a mistake today, Frank would take me aside tomorrow and we'd work on certain things. I learned, for instance, that when a man is on second and the score is tied, it's important to block a low throw rather than try to scoop it. If it gets by you, the game's over. Otherwise you should always have your right foot on the bag, unless the throw is off the base to the inside. Then you tag the runner.

"I was no gazelle, but I got the job done. But Casey would still ask me, 'If a guy is hurt, Moose, can you play third?' As long as he had the confidence in me, I'd try."

—MOOSE SKOWRON

"Casey would ask anyone with any credibility to help out. He had Gil Hodges teaching first base and giving us a lot of strategic advice. He had us give with the glove on balls to our backhand side. If you lunge at the ball, he said, you'll have stiff hands, but if you give you'll be relaxed."

—ED KRANEPOOL

"On a hot Sunday at old Busch Stadium in St. Louis. The Mets were in the field. Marvelous Marv [Throneberry] was holding down first base. This is like saying Willie Sutton works at your bank.

"It was the eighth inning of the first game of a doubleheader, and the Cardinals had Ken Boyer on first and Stanley Musial at third. Two were out. Boyer took a lead, then broke for second on the pitch. The throw to second from the Mets' catcher was, by some sort of miracle, perfect. It had Boyer beat by a mile, and the Cardinal runner, only half-way down, turned and tried to go back to first. The Mets' second baseman, Rod Kanehl, threw to Throneberry. Boyer was trapped.

"Standard operating procedure in a situation of this kind is for the man with the ball to chase the runner, but with one eye firmly fixed on the man on third. If he breaks for home, you're supposed to go after him and forget the other guy.

"So Boyer turned and started to run away from Throneberry. This seemed to

incense Marv. Nobody runs away from Marvin Throneberry. He took after Boyer with purpose. He did not even wink at Musial. Marvelous Marv lowered his head a little and produced wonderful running action with his legs. This amazed the old manager, Casey Stengel, who was standing on the top step of the Mets' dugout. It also amazed Mr. Musial, who was relaxing on third. Stanley's mouth opened. Then he broke for the plate and ran across it and into the dugout with the run that cost the Mets the game.''

—JIMMY BRESLIN, *Can't Anybody Here Play This Game?*

CASEY ON SECOND BASE

"Casey would tell a player like Felix Mantilla to cheat a step to his right because he could go to his left better. He didn't want to move a player over so far he couldn't get to his weak side. It was part of Casey's psychology: getting the most out of his players.''

—SOLLY HEMUS

"At the instructional camp Casey was grooming Bobby Richardson and me as the double-play combination. He was very big on quickness of the feet and balance. After we played catch, we played what he called 'quick catch.' It was a drill that was especially good for the second baseman turning the pivot. No matter where the ball was thrown, you had to get your feet and body in position so you could get rid of the ball very quickly. You were supposed to catch the ball with two hands and get rid of it. You'd do that for about ten minutes straight. The idea was to make the double play more quickly and work with your playing partner.''

—TONY KUBEK

I like [Jerry] *Coleman for a double play* [pivot] *. . . Could throw straight overhand and if it was an ordinary first baseman he never threw bad because he threw overhanded. If he threw sidearm the ball would sink into the ground.*

Then there was Mr. Frisch, which went to a university and could run fast besides. He was the first second baseman that didn't pedal backwards when they hit the ball down the line. He'd put his head down and commence running like in a race, and he'd beat the ball there.

[Nellie] *Fox played a good game in the field at second base, and he'd stand up at the plate and barber and keep the boys irritated. And he'd even walk by and step on the resin bag for our bats, and make the resin run out.*

RICHARDSON ON STENGEL

"I came up as a shortstop. Casey said, 'I have a good man at that position—you'd better learn to play second.' Frank Crosetti was the infield coach, and he did the coaching. He taught me to position myself closer to the bag on double-play situations. That way you can stay in position until the last second if a man is stealing and the batter is swinging. I also got help from Jerry Coleman and Snuffy Stirnweiss. But I didn't think I'd get to play. Norm Siebern and Jerry Lumpe were traded, and I wanted to be, too. Instead, they traded Billy Martin. 'O.K., kid, it's all yours now,' Casey told me."

"Casey often communicated with you in a roundabout way. I don't mean just his talking about nineteen other things and meaning just one that pertained to you. Sometimes he'd get to you by going through the press, and you'd read that Casey thought I wasn't playing deep enough at second—he thought I should play deeper because I was good at coming in on ground balls—or that I wasn't going to my right well enough. And other times he'd go through his coaches, like our infield coach, Frankie Crosetti.

"You might be standing at the cage during batting practice and Cro would come up to you and say, 'Casey and I were talking. . . .' One of the keys to making the double play at second base, which may be the most important thing you do as a second baseman, was to get to the bag on time to get the throw. One thing I learned was that if, normally, you'd play fifteen feet away from the base with a man on first, it would be better for you to play maybe two feet closer to the base. And then you don't have to break to the bag when the runner does, but you can wait to see what the hitter does, and still make it to the bag in time."

—BOBBY RICHARDSON

CASEY ON SHORTSTOP

Maybe we ain't got a name shortstop, but we sure gotta lot of them and if a feller can play good, I can always switch him around. Mantle was a shortstop, and if I hold him back waitin' for Rizzuter to get old, which was a tree-mendous player through the years, and I even played Collins in the outfield [instead of first base] *in the World Series, because he had a sore side and I didn't want 'em to bunt on him.*

[To sore-armed Phil Rizzuto in 1949]
Take your time. You know how to play shortstop and you know how to take care of yourself. Work out in the mornings at our field. When you feel like it, come over to the other field when we're playing there. But don't come over until you're ready. And remember you won't be put into the line-up until you ask me to put you in.

Rizzuto had somewhat hurt his arm . . . which had handicapped the club during the 1948 pennant race. He could go to his right very speedily, but I was told by some of the players at spring training that it had become pretty hard for him to throw a man out after he went way deep for a ball over toward third base.
I watched him in training camp and suggested that he loft the ball to get it over there. And he did whether I wanted him to or not. The big thing is not what the manager tells you, but what you do about it yourself. And he perfected a system in which he could get rid of the ball with an amazing quick throw. It would fly in the air, but he'd get rid of it so fast it would beat the runner. And that sometimes is better than an infielder who catches the ball, takes too long to throw it, and then throws a bullet over to first base.

A shortstop is the same thing as a quarterback out there. He's got to go and back up every play; he's got to watch every base; he's got to go out and take relays. Any place the ball is hit, he's got to have a spot he goes to. He has to go all over the ballpark.

KUBEK ON STENGEL

"On one pivot on a double play I had made a bad throw because I was watching the runner come in instead of looking at the first baseman. Casey had me pull the cap down over my eyes. 'O.K.,' he said, 'now I'm going to show you what you're doing. Now tell me where you're going to throw.' I couldn't see first base. 'If you can look and see the first baseman,' he said, 'you'll make the throw. You can only see the baserunner, so you can't see the first baseman.' It was like Baseball 101, but it worked.

"Frankie Crosetti did a lot with us, but I'm sure much of it came from Casey. He always taught you to think ahead. If you've just struck out and you go onto the field, you won't be in the right place at the right time if you're not thinking. And you have to be constantly thinking about situations. If I'm the shortstop, a man is on first, and the ball is hit to right field, where do I go? Second base. If the center fielder fields a hit with a man on first, I've got to be the cutoff man between the center fielder and the third baseman. Casey would talk about thinking these plays ahead so that it becomes automatic.

"He had one play that was very interesting. When you're the cutoff man on a ball hit to right with a man on first, instead of going to your usual cutoff position, you'd be closer to third. The hitter usually glances to see if the throw is high so that he can go into second. Or he'll look toward the cutoff man. Casey always had the cutoff spot vacant. Once the outfielder released the ball, then the shortstop would start running toward him. What Casey was trying to do was deceive the runner as he left the plate. He would look over his shoulder, see nothing and keep going. Meanwhile, the shortstop was running up on the ball and ready to throw it.

"I once trapped a popup three times in one season so that I could throw out a fast baserunner at second and have a slower one on first. That was the kind of play Casey taught. In a bunt situation, when runners are on first and second and the bunter pops it up, it's not an infield fly calling for an automatic out. Many people don't realize that. 'Trap it!' you could hear Casey yelling from the dugout. We got double plays that way I can't tell you how many times."

—TONY KUBEK

CASEY ON THIRD BASE

[When a third baseman let a grounder bounce off his glove for a two-base error]
Next time a ball is hit toward you, please don't touch it, because then my left fielder can come in and hold it to a single.

Tony Kubek. (NBL)

With a bad back you can't play third because you gotta dip too quick, see?

"[Gil] McDougald, tall, angular, red-faced, with an odd way of cocking his head to one side as though he had a wry neck, was an awkward-looking athlete but the kind of ballplayer Stengel loved. He had been an all-star second baseman in the Texas League the year before, but when Casey asked him in spring training if he could play third base [Casey already had Jerry Coleman and Billy Martin at second], McDougald said he'd be glad to give it a try. He proved so adept at the position that the Yankees traded away Billy Johnson soon after the season began."

—Robert W. Creamer, *Stengel*

[On McDougald]
A very awkward man, a wonderful man.

"I had a bad habit of breaking to my left and deflecting balls Eddie Miller could have had at short. I went up to Casey and asked him what I was doing wrong. He said, 'You just keep going and get everything you can regardless of whether they deflect off your glove or not.' And that's what I did."

—Sibby Sisti

"The key to playing proper third base is balance, so that you can go to the left, right, backwards and forwards. Don't lean too far forward. Don't be back on your heels. Have your arms relaxed. Have your glove down. I always had it around my knees, because it's easier to come up than go down. Assume everything that's hit to you is going to be a bad hop. Charge the ball. Play it on your hop rather than letting it play you. If I went to my left or right, I always tried to have the hands as close to the ground as possible."

—Andy Carey

CASEY ON THE OUTFIELD

Well, do you ever remember DiMaggio ever diving for a ball? He had an uncanny start. It looked like he could go after a ball at the sound of an echo.

[Told "Watch the angles, kid" when a ball caromed away from him in the minors]

Angles. If I wanted to learn to play the angles, I wouldn't be here, but down at Johnny Kling's pool hall.

"At Ebbets Field [in 1915] he had gotten into the habit of going out to the park early, borrowing three or four beat-up old practice balls from [Dan] Comerford's ball bag, and going out to right field, where he'd throw ball after ball against the wall, studying the way they bounced off it. He was learning to 'play the angles,' as Danny Shay had beseeched him to do when he was a rookie with Kansas City in 1910."

—CREAMER, *Stengel*

A fly ball goes out there and you got two fellas in the outfield sayin', 'I don't want it; you get it,' and they bunk heads. I ain't seen no one die on a ball field chasin' balls.

"One year Casey brought Joe DiMaggio to coach in spring training. He wasn't what you would call extroverted, but he was good. He told us that with a man on third and a fly ball that wasn't hit too deep, you shouldn't come in and catch the ball flat-footed. You should put on a burst of speed, catch it on the dead run, about face-high, and get rid of it as fast as you could. On grounders to the outfield with a man on second, you don't catch the ball two-handed. You should straddle it, reach down with your glove, and come up throwing. If it's do-or-die like that, you can't get down on one knee or field the ball like an infielder. With the bases empty, yes."

—JOHN BLANCHARD

MANTLE ON STENGEL

"I was just a kid shortstop, nineteen years old, and Stengel made me into an outfielder in a month.

"It was obvious as soon as I came up in 1951 that I wasn't going to continue playing shortstop. Casey told me, 'You're too fast and you have too good an arm and too much power to play shortstop.' What he didn't mention was that I'd made seventy-seven errors at short the previous season. We were in Arizona and he took me out to right field. He showed me the proper position: left hand on my knees and right hand on my sunglasses. 'As soon as you see the ball hit to you, flick them down,' he said.

"In my first game Ike [Ray] Boone hit one my way. I flicked down the glasses and lost the ball completely. It hit me right in the forehead. Gene

83

Woodling, who was playing outfield with me, came running over. 'Are the glasses broken?' he asked me. That was all he wanted to know.

"A few weeks later we played three exhibition games in New York with the Dodgers. Before the first one at Ebbets Field, Casey took me out to the short right-field wall. This time he gave me good advice: 'If the ball's hit at all good, it'll hit the wall or screen, so you might as well play shallow and catch the balls that aren't hit too good. Also, if you're not too close to the wall, the carom will come back to you and you can hold the batter to a single. If you're too close to the wall, the ball will bounce over your head.'

"I couldn't believe how much Casey knew about Ebbets Field. 'Did you play out here?' I asked him.

" 'Hell, yes,' he said. 'I was a good outfielder, too.' I'll never forget what he told the press the next day: 'The kid from Oklahoma thinks I was born at the age of sixty-two and started managing immediately.' "

—MICKEY MANTLE

[On playing right field in the Phillies' tiny park in 1920–21]
I had the wall behind me, the second baseman in front of me, the foul line on my left, and Cy Williams on my right. The only time I had to catch the ball was when it was hit right at me.

"Casey didn't like outfielders who casually fielded the ball instead of getting there early and setting their feet."

—HANK BAUER

"Casey thought relays were very important. He'd say, 'Lopez [former White Sox and Indians manager Al Lopez] will win ninety games and we'll win ninety games. If we can win two more with good relays, we'll win the pennant.' He stressed two things: having a trailer on the relay, and throwing the ball six feet to the left of the relay man. Most infielders are righthanded. If you throw the ball to their left, they'll be lined up to throw home when they get it."

—WHITEY HERZOG

When you throw them [relays] *low, the infielder has to bend down and loses a step in relaying the ball home. Throw it high and the relay home may get your man and you might win the game.*

(AP/WIDE WORLD PHOTOS)

Ron Swoboda. (UPI/BETTMANN)

SWOBODA SPEAKS

"One time, at Casey Stengel Field in St. Petersburg, he wanted to show us how to throw from the outfield. There were a couple of guys standing out in right field. I guess Casey was getting frustrated, so he picked up the ball and threw it. It almost hit him in the toes—didn't go two feet! 'That's the way I want you to throw it,' he said. 'Keep the ball down.'

"One of the things Casey taught you about playing the outfield was the importance of turning your back on the ball. He would talk to you about running to the place where you thought the ball was going to land. When you first start doing this, you're going to miss a few, but you'll get better at it. Eventually the ball will be there. It's a technique kids don't know about: picking up the ball, making your break, then turning and relocating the ball so that you get a better break on it. 'And you might need that helmet when you're learning it,' he said.

"The key was the first look at the ball. When it goes up, you don't turn away until you're pretty damn sure where it's going to land. You learn to ask yourself, Did he get a piece of it, is it jumping, or is it a ball you can get to comfortably?

" 'Practice the hardest things that you have to do,' Casey would say, 'the things that you don't do well. Turn your back on balls in practice that you don't have to. It'll just build this skill so that when you have to do it, you'll be able to.'

"[Swoboda made a diving, backhanded catch that was considered the key moment of the 1969 World Series and one of the greatest plays in postseason history.] The catch in the '69 Series was a condensation of a drill I used to do a lot under Casey. You stand 150 feet away from a guy with a fungo bat and you tell him to hit line drives to the left and right of you. You're going to have to move on a lot of them. He won't be able to hit line drives all the time. If he hits ground balls, then you practice charging them with the winning run on second or whatever situation you want to create. You bust your ass and get your footwork or body under control. You catch the ball with your feet the same way so that you're ready to get a more efficient release. If it's a line drive, you practice going for it or catching it on a hop or breaking back. It was the stuff you can win or lose a ballgame on. 'You're not going to get any better catching those lollipops hit by the pitcher before the game,' Casey said. 'Practice the plays you'll make with the game on the line.'

"He was the manager when we played in some peculiar old parks like Forbes and Crosley. His advice was always to go out there and fire some balls off the wall. Find out what the ball does when it goes down the line. Old Connie Mack Stadium had those corrugated aluminum things, so you'd see what the ball did when it hit the metal and the fence. Crosley had the terrace. Casey went out there with me and showed me what to do with it. He had played in the park and he said you had to play up in the incline. You didn't want to run up to it. If you played up on it, you'd know you were on an incline. The other part of it was, you had to allow your body to slow down when you moved up the hill. You're going upward, so you're kind of catching up with the ball. You don't have to move as fast as you normally would. If you accelerated, you'd move right into the hill. He told us to figure out the wind. The more you could become familiar with, the less the new ballpark would affect you. It was all common sense.

"He told us about sunglasses, too. In a new ballpark, find the sun. See where it is and how it hits you. Go out there with your glasses on. I cost us a game in 1965 because I screwed up. He always said to wear your sunglasses when you don't think you'll need them. There's a mechanic to getting them down pat so that you feel comfortable seeing the ball through them. So you take fly balls with them down and don't wait until you need to wear them and haven't in five days.

"Anyway, it happened in the old St. Louis ballpark. We were leading 3–0, bottom of the ninth, with two outs. It had rained off and on and the tarp was pretty soaked. Finally the clouds started to disappear over the third-base dugout. Suddenly the sun was out and sitting right over the stadium. But I didn't have my glasses on. Dal Maxvill was batting with two outs and the bases loaded. Larry Bearnarth was pitching and doing a hell of a job. I thought, 'The only ball that could bother me is a dying quail over second.' And the worst that could happen, happened: Maxvill quailed on me. I lost it in the sun, it got by me, and three runs scored.

"I came up the next inning—now it was in extra innings—and popped up. We started running into the outfield for the bottom half of the inning. My batting helmet, one of those fiberglass jobs you could crush, was lying on the top step, face down. I kind of focused on it, took a running leap, and jumped on it. And my foot stuck.

"I was trying to shake it off, and Stengel saw me. He had busted his wrist and had a cast on. I panicked a little. 'Jesus Christ,' I thought, 'he's going to crack me with that cast and here I am stuck on my helmet!'

"Instead he ran up the steps and grabbed me by the shirt with his good hand. 'When you dropped that fucking fly ball, I didn't throw your watch on the floor in the locker room,' he said, 'so I don't want you busting up this equipment when you fuck up. You're out of the game.' I pulled off the helmet and went downstairs and cried in the locker room. We lost the game. It was the low point of my major-league career."

—RON SWOBODA

[On Swoboda]

Amazing strength, amazing power. He can grind the dust out of the bat. He will be great, super, wonderful. Now if he can only learn to catch a fly ball. . . .

Casey at the plate.   (NBL)

5

CASEY ON BATTING

OR

"Not Too Hard, Not Too Easy, Just Tra-La-La."

STENGEL LIKED A MANY-FACETED hitting attack—homers, bunts, hit-and-run, timely pinch-hitting all through the game. He liked fly balls in small parks and grounders in big ones. Above all, he insisted on making contact. But his views on hitting could never be quite so neatly capsulized.

If Ted Williams could see the ball so good up at the plate, then why don't umpires stand sideways to call balls and strikes?

The big men at the present time, they go for home runs. Of course, they outsmart themselves many a time, when they've left three men on and two men on. They fail with men on third and second. They're afraid to just meet the ball, and they strike out.

"I used to try to hit every ball over the fence, and I'd strike out and get mad as hell. 'You dumb son of a bitch, you're trying to hit every ball to the courthouse steps,' Casey told me. He kept trying to get me to meet the ball. He used to stand on the steps of the dugout yelling, 'Butcher boy, goddamn it, butcher boy.' He wanted me to 'meat' the ball.

"Because I had a bad right knee, I had to uppercut balls when I was batting lefthanded. The pitchers knew this and would strike me out on high, inside pitches. 'How dumb can you be?' Casey yelled at me one time after I struck out on three of those pitches. 'Lay off them and take walks. Wait for pitches you can hit.'

"On the next at bat after I homered, they'd start me out by throwing at my right knee. I had to jump back, and it was painful. Casey thought I should put a steel guard on the knee so I wouldn't have to jump. I never used one, but I did

92

learn to just turn on the knee. That way the pitch would hit me on the back of the leg and wouldn't hurt as much."

—MICKEY MANTLE

" 'Butcher boy' had another meaning: It meant chopping down on the ball. Any time Casey wanted to move up a runner, especially if he was on third, he'd yell 'butcher boy' to get a high-bouncing ground ball."

—JACK LANG

"He had a fake bunt-and-swing play. 'Now I want a butcher boy,' he'd shout. 'Hit it on home plate, bounce it up in the air.' "

—DON ZIMMER

"Casey told me, 'Don't strike out with two strikes. Use the whole field—butcher boy.' He wanted you to hit down on the ball—chopping wood—hit grounders and line drives.

"I have a photograph of him instructing me to hit. He was fooling around with my knees to tell me about weight distribution. His view of technical hitting was basically everybody's view. You should bend over at the waist and get the weight on your back foot before you stride in. Then you transfer your weight as you stride forward. You grip the bat with your fingertips; that's where you should get the calluses. If you hold the bat too far back, you'll tighten your wrists and forearms, you'll lock up and you won't get good whip action. Normally, the shorter your stride, the better, because you get better balance. If you take a longer stride, you're off balance, and if the pitcher changes speeds you're in trouble. With a shorter stride, you can stay back on the ball longer.

"I look at that picture of Casey and me, and I say, 'What a stupid ass I am!' You see, I never got him to sign it."

—ED KRANEPOOL

The Youth of America, you bring them in and they swing as hard as they can and you just tell them to m-e-e-t the ball, and they look at you. They don't know their hitting area, so they swing at balls they can't hit, and when you protect them [by benching them against tough pitchers], *they say, 'The fellow isn't playing me.'*

"I took Paul Waner's place in the outfield after a few months. Casey taught us a lot about hitting. He said to have patience at the plate. You gotta be relaxed, but

93

you gotta be ready. Just lay the bat on your shoulder and wait for the ball. He said you're better off guessing for a curve than a fastball because it makes you wait longer. I did—I was a good curveball hitter. They never threw me curves. They threw me high fastballs inside.

"Casey said don't try to pull every ball. Hit 'em down the right-field line, hit 'em down the left-field line. I did—I changed. Wherever the ball was pitched, I could jump up in the air and hit it. I was the best hit-and-run man in Kansas City. I can stand up there against anybody and still get the bat on the ball, and I'm in my eighties.

"Casey liked to hit-and-run because it helps the team. If they have a good double-play combination, they can't get the man who's going to second. I used to watch the second baseman and shortstop and see who was covering and hit into his space. I was like Willie Keeler."

—FRENCHY BORDAGARAY

"He was always telling us to watch the ball and not overswing. If you overswing, you pull your head out. His main theory was that if you couldn't see the ball, you couldn't hit it."

—MARV THRONEBERRY

[After the Mets' George Altman won a game with a homer into a shipyard]
Over a building, over a yard, over a ship, and into the wild blue yonder.

[After Mets minor leaguer Ron Swoboda homered to win an exhibition game]
You wanna win a game like this, but you wonder if maybe it ain't good to watch a young fella like that hit it over a building.

I've been to that new park in Anaheim where they've got that young fella [Rick Reichardt] *they're calling the new Mickey Mantle. He knocks the ball out of sight and then strikes out three times in a row but he's the Youth of America and the youth always comes through.*

"When I hit fly balls, Casey would say to me, 'Young fella, there ain't no bad hops up there.' "

—HANK BAUER

Ed Kranepool and Casey.   (UPI/BETTMANN)

[On Johnny Mize]

The older he got, the better he got. Know why? I'll tell ya. He knew he could hit for distance. Sometimes it's better not to. So he put that in his mind and went on the size of the park he was in. He'd come up, pinch-hit, and there'd be three men on base. They'd pitch the ball in on him, and he'd go the other way. Not too hard, not too easy. He'd just go 'butcher boy.' Just chop at the ball. The same way a butcher chops at a piece of meat.

If a man can't hit a curve, why wouldn't he get the batting practice pitcher to throw him curves instead of just seeing how far he can hit it at noon?

"Bill Dickey and Charlie Keller worked with me. I was lunging at certain pitches. Bill Dickey would say, 'Pick up your heel and then stride.' That would make you wait.

"I led the league in hitting into double plays. Casey said, 'If you don't learn to hit to right, you'll wind up in the minors.' That awakened me, so I'd take two shots to right with men on base. Casey helped me become a better all-around ballplayer.

"He kidded me about hitting to right in one World Series. The bases were loaded with one out, and he said, 'Take a shot to right.' Roger Craig threw me outside and low, and I pulled it and hit a grand slam. When I came into the dugout, Casey said, 'That's the way to hit it to left field.' "

—MOOSE SKOWRON

"I could not hit lefthanders, but one day in spring training Casey took a bat and said, 'Now you've got this protected, and that protected, and over here protected— and if he throws three strikes out here, what the heck, get 'em next time.' Get 'em next time? Thanks, Case.

"One time in spring training, we had the hit-and-run on, and Carl Erskine threw me a curve and I struck out into a double play. I came back to the bench and Casey said, 'Next time, tra-la-la.' I didn't know what tra-la-la meant, but next time I got up, I hit a line drive, right into a double play. When I sat down, Casey came over and said, 'Like I told you, tra-la-la.' "

—WHITEY HERZOG

"If you swung too hard, he'd yell out, 'Not too hard, not too easy, just tra-la-la.' "

—HANK BAUER

"Hickman took three straight strikes, was out, and the inning was over.

"In the clubhouse Stengel leaned out from his small office, looked toward his distraught outfielder, and sang an old ditty.

" 'Oh you can't improve your average with the bat on your shoulder,

" 'Oh you can't improve your average with the bat on your shoulder,

" 'Oh you can't improve your average with the bat on your shoulder tra la la la la la la la la.'

" 'I learned that song,' said Casey, 'from Uncle Robby [former Dodger manager Wilbert Robinson]. Only I can't teach it to Hickman.'

" 'Why doesn't he get off my back,' screamed the usually mild-mannered Hickman. 'Swing, swing, swing. That's all I ever hear from him.' "

—MAURY ALLEN, *Now Wait a Minute, Casey*

"Stengel was called out on strikes. When he came back to the bench muttering imprecations against the umpire, [John] McGraw showed him scant sympathy.

" 'Was the last pitch good enough to hit?' queried McGraw.

" 'It was wide,' explained Case.

" 'Maybe so, but you should have offered at it just the same. Never take a chance on the third one when it's hittable.'

"Stengel now gives his [Boston] Bees the same advice."

—HOWELL STEVENS OF THE *Boston Post* in *The Sporting News*

We got too many men strikin' out, too many men left on bases, too many one-run losses. If I can keep you from strikin' out twelve, fifteen times with men on third, I'd probably be more satisfied or near satisfied.

"Casey asked me to change my hitting in 1955. I used an open stance, and I proceeded to use a closed stance after that. His reasoning was that if I always pulled the ball to the left side of the diamond, the baserunner could rarely go from first to third. With the closed stance I started to hit the ball to center and right, which allowed the runner to easily go from first to third."

—GIL McDOUGALD

It would be nice to be able to carry twelve pitchers, but you've got to leave room on your bench for some pinch-hitters too.

There was another big reason why I platooned with relief pitchers. I like good pinch-hitters. I believe that with a lively ball you've got to be an attacker. If I've got a good pinch-hitter, I hate to have him stay on the bench with men on the bases in an early inning. He may end the game right there. He may make them take out their pitcher—a good pitcher that would otherwise have gone nine innings—because he popped him at the right time.

97

"When Casey said, 'Wait a minute,' you knew you'd be pinch-hit for."
—ENOS SLAUGHTER

"The first words that come to mind are, 'Hold that gun.' That meant Enos Slaughter was going to hit for you."
—BOBBY RICHARDSON

[When Yogi Berra called the park and told trainer Gus Mauch that he would be staying home with a bad cold]
You call Mr. Berra right back, and tell him to come to the park anyway—I might want him as a pinch-hitter.

"He demonstrated, almost daily, how games could be won by protecting even the good hitters from their one weakness. It was Stengel who showed them that your top pinch-hitter should be wheeled in at the first opportunity to break the game open, instead of being husbanded until the late innings."
—EDWARD LINN

"He told me how to hit in the Polo Grounds when I joined the Mets. 'Use both lines and never hit to center.' That made perfect sense, because the Polo Grounds were short down the foul lines and deep to center. I wasn't a home-run hitter, but I had seven that season for a career high. The other reason Casey said to hit down the foul lines was that double-play balls are usually hit to the shortstop and second baseman. So his advice was good for any park."
—RICHIE ASHBURN

"If you miss, it's only a foul ball, but if you get it in, it's a double. If the fielders move over to protect the lines you have more room in left center and right center for hits."
—VETERAN PLAYER PAUL WANER, using Stengel's blessing to advise rookie Tommy Holmes to hit down the foul lines [Holmes went on to lead the National League in hits, homers, and doubles in 1945 and bat over .300 five times.]

"At one point, after repeatedly using a big windup before throwing the ball, [Patsy] Flaherty quick-pitched, sudddenly throwing without a windup, a practice now illegal but at that time within baseball law. The pitch not only took Stengel by surprise, it hit him in the chest and knocked him down. He got up angrily, but the old pitcher

said calmly, 'Kid, I just wanted to give you a lesson. Never take your eye off the ball.' "

—Robert W. Creamer, *Stengel*

"[Kid] Elberfeld showed Stengel how to stand close to the plate at bat so that he could get himself hit with a pitched ball when it was especially desirable to get to first base, and how to defray suspicion that you'd gotten yourself hit on purpose by throwing your bat angrily toward the mound and moving threateningly toward the pitcher, shouting and cursing."

—Creamer, *Stengel*

[The Giants traded Stengel to Boston after he hit two homers for his team's only wins in the 1923 World Series.]

It's lucky I didn't hit three home runs in three games in the series, or McGraw would've traded me to the Three–I League.

It was rougher then. Now, when a pitcher happens to get a ball close to a hitter, the hitter comes back to the bench and says, 'I think he was throwing at me.' Boys, when I broke in, you just knew they were throwing at you. The first month I was in the league, I spent three weeks on my back at the plate.

"What Charles Dillon Stengel proceeded to say was that this is the year [1961] Mantle will break Babe Ruth's 34-year-old record of sixty home runs.

" 'Now I'll tell you why,' he continued. '(1) His attitude. Them people must have gave him a real nice contract. (2) He'll be hitting against tiring pitchers late in the season on account of the longer schedule. (3) Why shouldn't he break it? He's got more power than Staleen.'

"Ole Case had an afterthought. . . . 'And this park out there where one of them new teams [Los Angeles Angels] plays will give him chances he never had before. If a fella like him just nudges the ball, it's a home run.' There may be substance in much of what the Glendale Banker says.

"Old Case had another observation. . . . 'Maris will help beat the intentional pass. They ain't going to pass him to get to Mantle. If he can go all the way this year, and stay hot, that'll keep Mantle on his toes, make him more choosy and he won't strike out so much.' "

—*The Joe Williams Reader* [Homers indeed flew out of parks in the 1961

99

expansion season. Mickey Mantle had 54 and Roger Maris—possibly benefiting from hitting in front of Mantle—set a new record with 61.]

Why ain't there any heavy bats around anymore, like the one Joe Jackson used, and Hank Gowdy used after him. You know that Jackson was the only one who ever hit a ball clear out of the Polo Grounds, over the roof and all, until they brought in the lively ball? Jackson hit that lump of coal with a heavy bat, and people who saw it ain't sure it's come down yet, though that's maybe thirty-five years ago.

Now the owner of the Sacramento ball club had a room where they kept mementos of the ball club, and they kept the big bat his fella had used, which I can't remember his name. They brought out the bat one day, polished as mahogany. My fellas hefted it, the young kids, strong fellas they was, but they pick up this heavy bat with the thick handle. 'Ugh,' they say. They don't like it none.

But I got one fella to use it and he became a very good hitter with the bat.

You know something, the heavy bat, if you could get anybody to use it, would be the answer to the slider. Balls that come in on the fists now, either break the bat or turn up with dinky grounders to the infield. With the big handle there would be so many balls popping over the infield the slide pitcher would go nuts. But no, the boys find out what weight Musial uses and that's for them.

[Asked if Babe Ruth used a heavy bat]
He could have used his sleeve, or a rolled up copy of the Police Gazette. Wouldn't have made a bit of difference.

"When Casey Stengel managed the Braves from the late '30s into the early '40s, a hitter complaining about the wind would get a chilling, sarcastic response from the Old Perfesser. 'Y–e–s,' he would say, dragging out the affirmative characteristically, 'it is a shame. Mr. Hornsby played here only one season (1928), and he hit only .387.' "

—BOB BROEG, *Baseball from a Different Angle*

They win with the Yanks over there and we don't with the Mets over here. RBI. You know what that means? Runs

Batted In. That's the bigest thing wrong with this club, it needs more RBI. If you don't make the runs, you don't make the scoreboard and that's a mighty expensive scoreboard they got out there; seems a waste of money not keeping it goin'.

[Asked about the designated hitter]
Of course I'm for it. I've been doin' it all my life, ain't I? . . .
Sure, I used to believe in takin' pitchers out. I believed in takin' other guys out too no matter what inning it was. I took [Clete] *Boyer out once in the second inning of a World Series in Pittsburgh, before he ever came up to bat, and got hell for it, remember?*
I did it because they had scored three–four runs in the first inning. So I put in a pinch-hitter. Why in hell not? I'm behind, ain't I? How in hell am I gonna catch 'em in nine innings if I don't try to? It's too late to catch 'em tomorrow. The guy I put in for Boyer was Dale Long, who used to play outfield and first base for Pittsburgh. The fella hit a line drive that was caught. We scored some runs anyway, but we lost. Remember the big smell they made about it? They said it was Boyer's first World Series, and how could I be so mean and take him out?

When we are getting some hits we aren't getting them when we have somebody on the bases. It's very aggravating. But maybe it's better to see them left there than not getting them on at all. If they keep getting on you got to figure one of these days they'll be getting home. Or it could be one of these years, you know.

[Muscled out of batting practice as a rookie, Stengel showed up at the park the next day and handed each teammate a printed card.]
HI. MY NAME IS CHARLES DILLON "DUTCH" STENGEL. I WOULD LIKE TO TAKE BATTING PRACTICE. [His nickname was "Dutch," for "Deutsch," or German, before he became known as "Casey."]

They go for the loft hitter now. The batter tries to hit a long fly with men on third and second and the infield in. In olden times, with a dead ball, he wouldn't be such a great hitter, because he'd just be hitting high flies. When I started in the big leagues the pitcher would pitch to make them hit a ball in the outfield. He didn't worry about the home run, with the best sluggers hitting only fifteen or twenty a year. He'd look back at me, a green outfielder, and give me a little sign to go right or go to the left, and he'd make them loft a high pitch. But now the outfield is a dangerous place to have them hit, with the lively ball and with the parks in many places being smaller, because of the extra seats that have been built in. The ball caroms off the modern concrete walls much sharper than it used to off the old wooden fences. Or it goes in the stands, and the best outfielder just can't get up in the grandstand and catch that home run for you.

"Johnny Blanchard went up there pinch-hitting and took two of the hardest swings you've ever seen. Missed both of them. I think the pitcher was throwing knuckleballs or curves. Finally, Casey said, 'Hold that gun'—time out. Casey went to the on-deck circle and called him over there. 'I want you to butcher boy,' he said, yelling and demonstrating. When he was demonstrating, he stepped on Blanchard's foot—spiked him—and they had to take him out for a pinch-hitter."

—TONY KUBEK

[When Mantle kicked a water cooler after striking out]
It ain't the water cooler which is gettin' you out.

CASEY ON BUNTING

Casey Stengel loved to bunt. He was saddened that the lively ball and harder turf made bunting tougher and shifted the emphasis to baserunning, but he never entirely gave up on bunting.

I think the bunting situation is terrible. Nobody can bunt anymore, or they say they can't. It's as easy as choppin' wood.

"Stengel has a theory that just about the most effective way of bunting is to hit directly downward—he calls it chopping wood—so that (1) the catcher will be the *only man around to make a play and (2) will be able only to throw out the batter at first while other runners advance."*

— GILBERT MILLSTEIN, *The New York Times Magazine*

"Casey worked with a lot of guys on bunting. Before the first pitch of my first spring-training game he told me to fake a bunt. 'You get him in. Now you slap in by him,' he said. 'You're 1-for-1. Now he's afraid to come in and you bunt. You're 2-for-2. Now you open your hip and double down the right-field line. You're 3-for-3.'

"Mantle came up to me and said, 'You haven't even batted yet, and you're 3-for-3.' Casey had been making a point: Against a lumbering pitcher you bunt. He wasn't saying that in so many words. He was teaching me to think for myself."

— TONY KUBEK

[When Warren Spahn shut out the Mets]
You would think they would bunt on a forty-three-year-old man.

"Casey began talking to them about the niceties of bunting, and how on a squeeze play the hitter should bunt down the third-base line if the pitcher is lefthanded, or down the first-base line if he is righthanded."

— HARRY T. PAXTON

"Casey always emphasized not to swing too hard. After Mantle hit a home run, he'd tell him to drag one to confuse the opposition. When I was managing the All-Star team, Mantle hit one over the right-field fence. The next time up, he asked me, 'Do you want me to drag one?' He was serious. I said, 'Hell, no, hit another over the fence.' "

— AL LOPEZ

CASEY IN CLEVELAND

Now here [a big game against the Indians, on September 17, 1951] comes one of the most beautifully executed plays I've ever seen. Rizzuto is at the plate. He's a pretty good bunter, and might be able to squeeze DiMaggio home with the winning run. But [Bob] Lemon is a great pitcher at fielding his position, and so is [Jim] Hegan, the catcher—they generally kept us from bunting too much.

Cleveland is ready for the squeeze. [Al] Rosen, the third baseman, says to DiMaggio off third base, 'I think this man is going to bunt.' DiMaggio says, 'It wouldn't surprise me,' and turns away with that cold stare he has.

Lemon pitches a strike to Rizzuto. Then he winds up again, and as he winds up he's watching to see if DiMaggio starts breaking for home. If DiMaggio does, then Lemon will pitch out so Rizzuto can't bunt, and DiMaggio will be tagged at the plate.

But good old Joe just stands there till the moment Lemon opens his fingers to release the ball, and then he makes his break. The pitch is inside, which makes it tough for Rizzuto to bunt down the first-base line, away from a righthanded pitcher, but he lays it down there anyhow.

The bunt was so perfect and DiMaggio had such a big jump that the Cleveland catcher just turned and started walking off the field before Joe even crossed the plate. Lemon ran over and picked up the ball, and when he saw it was impossible to make a play, he tried to throw the ball over the grandstand.

6

CASEY ON SPEED AND
BASERUNNING

OR

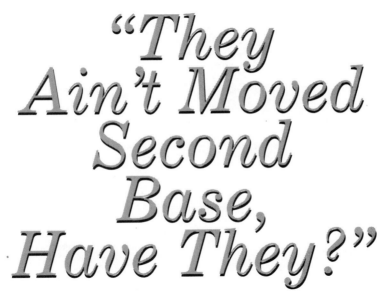

*"They
Ain't Moved
Second
Base,
Have They?"*

Joe DiMaggio slides into home.   (AP/WIDE WORLD PHOTOS)

RUN, SHEEP, RUN! That was one of Casey's favorite expressions. He felt everyone should learn to run the bases. Though the Yankees rarely had base-stealing speed, they did have outstanding baserunners—players who studied pitchers and fielders, improved their footwork, knew when to go for the extra base, and could go from first to third or second to home or even first to home as well as any players. If they couldn't run well, Casey taught them to.

Look at him [Joe DiMaggio], *he's always watching the ball. He isn't watching second base. He isn't watching third base. He knows they haven't been moved. He isn't watching the ground, because he knows they haven't built a canal or swimming pool since he was last there. He's watching the ball and the outfielder, which is the one thing that is different on every play.*

"*Casey taught baserunning better than anyone. Say you're leading off third and a righthanded batter is up. When the hitter is taking, you jump from foul to fair territory as the pitcher releases the ball. That way you can take a second lead, because the batter is directly between you and the catcher and obstructs the view. You can do that on suicides or double steals. On the double steal, with a man breaking from first, the catcher is taught to freeze the runner on third, then throw to second. With the obstructed view, you were five steps closer to the plate than you would have been in foul territory.*

"*If the catcher throws to third, you learn to let the throw hit you on the back and deflect away. I got hit three times and scored each time one season. You look over your shoulder, baiting him to throw. If the throw is low, you slide; if the throw is high, go in standing up.*"

—TONY KUBEK

CRAIG, CAREY, AND KRANEPOOL

"There was one thing I remember Casey doing the first day of spring training with the Mets. He would take the whole team to the on-deck circle and then walk them around the bases. It was kind of comical to the media. Here he had all these rejects and expansion-club players and he was going to show them where the bases were: 'This is where you wait before you hit, this is where you stand up to hit, this is where you stand if you get a base hit.' But that wasn't what he was doing at all. Unfortunately, the writers weren't always close enough to hear what he said. He was saying, 'When you're on the on-deck circle, here's what you look for. You want to watch that pitcher. What's he throwing? How good a fastball, how good a curveball, what he's throwing in certain situations? You're watching the base coach to see what signs he gives, what signs you can pick up from the catcher. Is the umpire a lowball umpire or highball umpire?'

"When we went from the on-deck circle to home plate, he said, 'This is where all the action is. You gotta cross home plate to win.' He'd actually step on home plate and cross it. He said it so simple, but he meant it: This is what it's all about.

"Then he talked about how you get signs, how you watch the pitcher and what he's throwing. 'A man singles to right field. Is there one out or two? Am I supposed to bunt him? If I am, is there a lefthanded pitcher or a righthanded pitcher? Is he a good fielder or a bad fielder? Is the third baseman playing in?'

"Then he'd take us down the line. 'Come down the line and hit the base like this [on the inside left corner with his left foot, cutting across with his right to face second]. If you can do that and do it again, you'll save twelve feet goin' from first to third.'

"Now he was lecturing to us on first. 'Watch the pitcher's move. Can you steal on him? When you steal, your left foot should go in front of your right foot on your first step. But if you're just taking a lead, your left foot should go behind your right foot on your first step. You back off the base. That way you can always move back toward first if the pitcher throws over. If you were swinging your left foot in front of your right when he threw over, you were stuck because you had no weight distribution and you couldn't get back.'

"Then there was this looking drill he'd used with the Yankees. 'Look around at the outfielders. Can you run on them? See where the outfielders are playing. If the ball is hit in the alleys, how good an arm have the center fielder and the right fielder got? Can I make it to third? Look around the infielders. When you get to the third baseman, the third-base coach will give you a signal. If he doesn't the batter might.'

"Then he'd go to second. You try to pick up signs from the catcher to relay to the hitter. You look to the outfield. Base hit, how good an arm, can I score in certain situations? If the ball's hit to your left, you can go to third. If it's hit in the hole between third and short, you have to wait until it goes through.

"At third, 'Is the infield playing in with one out? Can I score on a ground ball? I can tag up and score on a long fly ball. Who's the best defensive infielder? Make sure it's hit through the infield before you score. If it's a high chopper, you can make it if you've thought about the play ahead of time.'

"It was so good for us, but the media made a big spectacle of it where it was not."

—COMPOSITE OF DESCRIPTIONS BY ROGER CRAIG, ANDY CAREY, AND ED KRANEPOOL

You can see how that Aaron runs halfway to center field on singles to left? . . . if the throw's . . . on one side or the other of second base he keeps going.

Stealing bases isn't so very important now. The big thing is to know how to handle yourself trying to get from first to third when the ball is hit.

"Stengel would not easily forgive a man who got doubled up on a hit-and-run play—that is, was doubled at first on a line drive or a fly ball. He did not see any reason why the runner, busy as he was trying to reach second, could not give a quick glance back toward the plate to make sure the ball was hit safely."

—MICKEY MANTLE

[On the speedy 1942 Cardinals, who won 43 of their last 51 games to steal the pennant from Brooklyn]
Those jack-rabbits from St. Louis are coming.

You ask me what kind of ball club I'd want, one with power or one with speed, and I'd say, well, a lot of power but not

too much, and a lot of speed but not too much. The best club is the versatile club, the one that has a homer hitter here and a bunter there, a fastball pitcher here and a change-of-pace pitcher there. That way, the other team never knows what's going to hit it next.

CUB SECOND BASEMAN JOHNNY EVERS [to the rookie Stengel after he slid in spikes high]: One more time, rookie. One more time like that, and you eat this [the ball].

STENGEL: That's the way I slid in the bushes, Evers, and that's the way I'll slide up here. My name is Stengel. Take a good look at me, so you'll know me the next time you see me. I'm going to be around for a long time.

> *"Casey always felt you had to get the first step right to steal a base. He taught you to turn your right foot and get your body moving toward second in one motion— a kind of rhythm. You were supposed to understand and study the pitcher. 'When is he gonna throw to first?' Casey would ask. 'What does he move first: his foot, his head?' If you didn't pick up on the pitcher's moves, he got testy.*
>
> —SOLLY HEMUS

We got clean uniforms if you get 'em dirty. Why, the owners is just dyin' to have you get 'em dirty; I like to see 'em dirty. There's laundries. You tear a uniform, they're just waitin' to take it right off and give you another one.

> *"Casey was very practical about baserunning. He said to me, 'How many bunt singles did you get? Seven? You've got the speed to get five more. That's a .255 average instead of a .245 average—another $3,000 in salary.' It was like him telling a pitcher that if he developed a change-up, he'd be 15-5 instead of 10-10 and would make $50,000."*
>
> —ROD KANEHL

> *Some coaches would say that you should use the third-base coach when going from first to third. Working for Casey, I never told them that. Players should use their own judgment, based on knowing the game situation and the outfielder's arm. You should look around. If the right fielder is playing in right-center, you know you can go to third on a ball down the line. Mantle, McDougald, Collins, Kubek—I never had to tell them.*

"One of Casey's principles was that you should never get doubled off base on a line drive to an infielder. We'd yell, 'Watch the line drive!' Especially with a man on third. If a guy's on third, he can walk home when the ball gets through the infield."

— FRANK CROSETTI

"Casey was the best manager I ever saw for getting guys in from third on a flyball. He would take me out to third base and jump up and down and then he would say 'Now!' and push me toward home. It got to where I was pretty good at getting a jump off third base.

"He taught me one play I used all the time. There's one man out, a man on third, infield in, and a fast runner at the plate. The baserunner takes a walking lead, and when the batter hits a ground ball, he takes off for the plate. If the ball's hit to the fielder's left, he'll have to turn before throwing and the runner might score. Even if he's thrown out, the batter can steal second and you'll still have a runner in scoring position. We won two or three games a year on that play."

— WHITEY HERZOG

Some of my players think he's [Enos Slaughter] *a show-off. That's because every time they see him he's running.*

"One day we were playing the Tigers at their place in Lakeland, and I hit what should have been a double off the right-field wall—only, I tripped over first base and sprained my ankle. Lying there in pain, I looked up and saw Casey's face.

" 'Well, I'll be goddamned,' he says. 'You've been playing baseball all your life, and you still don't know where first base is at.' "

— HERZOG, *White Rat*

That shortstop for Los Angeles [Maury Wills] *is a bright baserunner. He gets a big lead and takes off. He knows it's ninety feet to the next base and he doesn't run with his head down. He takes a look at where the ball is heading and figures which fella is gonna to make the tag and on which side of the base. Then, he makes one of them slick slides and he's there before you can put the ball on him.*

It was a remarkable thing. Cobb would put on the hit-and-run and he'd never stop at first base. He'd go right on to second—an' where's the right fielder gonna throw the ball? There's only one place; he's got to throw it to second base with the shortstop covering.

So when the right fielder gets over his surprise, he throws to second base an' Cobb slides on his backside an' wraps his legs around the fella. So how's he gonna throw the ball home now, which is where the other runner is because he didn't stop at third base, either? An' it's a run scored an' it's a great play.

Tried it myself once. Know what happened? They got me at second base an' got the other fella at the plate an' my manager said maybe I shouldn't try that play anymore.

"It was while he was with the Giants that he convinced Bill Klem, the toughest umpire in the business, it was too wet to play a game. John McGraw had been trying for half a game to convince Klem the game should be called off without results, and was finally resigned to going through with it. Then Casey spoke up:

" 'Do you want this called off, Mac?' he asked.

"McGraw asked him what in hell he thought he had been arguing with Klem about [since the Giants were losing].

" 'All right, Mac. That's all I wanted to know,' said Casey and walked out on the field.

"He waded down to first base, took a crouching start and sped toward second. As he approached the bag he took off and made a head-first slide that ploughed up the soft ground for yards. Then he went dripping back to first and did it all over again.

"Klem came charging out and told him to cut out the foolishness, that he was ruining the diamond.

" 'Now, Mr. Klem,' said Casey placatingly. "I'm just taking my sliding practice, that's all. The team takes batting practice and fielding practice and I don't know of any rule to prevent me from taking my sliding practice, do you?'

"Klem called off the game."

—RICHARDS VIDMER, *New York Tribune*

If a man has five good points, why shouldn't he work on the sixth point that can make him better? How many times have you seen a man practice scoring from third on a fly? How often can you practice it in a game? You gotta hit a triple,

112

*right? But in batting practice, you can go down there every
time after you hit. . . .
Some of 'em complain that they can't get the signs on this or
that play, but why do you have to see the coach? Why don't
you know yourself, while you're on deck, what kind of an
arm the outfielder has, what I'll do if the batter doubles,
what I'll do if he triples, this is probably what they'll want.
Then you won't be so shocked and taken by surprise when
the sign is on.*
[On running a base] *Why do you have to look at the coach?
Second base is right where it always was, they ain't moved
it, have they? And there's no hills on the basepath or obstacle
courses, is there?*

"One time Mickey didn't run out a fly ball. When he got back to the dugout,
Casey asked him in front of me, Bobby Richardson, and Jerry Lumpe: 'Is your
leg bothering you?' When Mickey said no, Casey replaced him in the outfield. That
wasn't for Mickey. If he does that to Mantle, who had won the Triple Crown,
what does he do to us? It was Casey's psychology."

—TONY KUBEK

*There used to be more base-stealing, of course. One reason
they eventually cut out a lot of it was that most men, when
they tried to steal bases, would get thrown out half the time.
Then you've wasted half your hits. A base stealer is a
valuable man for the club only when he makes it almost
every time—the way Max Carey used to for Pittsburgh and
the way* [Luis] *Aparicio does for the White Sox today.*

*It's very simple how not to get picked off second with that ol'
hidden-ball trick. You just don't leave the bag until the
pitcher steps on the rubber, because it's a balk if he gets up
there without the ball.*

[Casey won the first game of the 1923 World Series with an inside-the-park
ninth-inning homer. As he rounded second, a pad in one shoe protecting his
bruised heel shifted, leaving Stengel with the feeling that his shoe was about to
come off—"Go, legs, go; drive this boy round the bases," he told his legs—and

left the writers with the impression that the thirty-three-year-old veteran was gimping around the bases. By the time he slid home, Stengel had created a scene for all time.]

It's a problem for a man of my age, what with a pair of what could be called stagnant legs and because of the fact that my shoe came apart halfway around second base, causing me to stumble a lot and just barely beat the throw to the plate. Oh, but beat it I did, and game one was ours. It caused that writer Damon Runyon to compose some beautiful words about how it was done.

[Runyon's story in the *New York American* appeared under the banner headline STENGEL'S HOMER WINS FOR GIANTS, 5–4, and the sub-heads, 60,000 Frantic Fans Screech as Casey Beats Ball to Plate. Warped Legs, Twisted, Bent in Years of Campaigning, Last Until He Reaches Goal. The copy began:]

This is the way old "Casey" Stengel ran yesterday afternoon, running his home run home.

This is the way the old "Casey" Stengel ran running his home run home in a Giant victory by a score of 5 to 4 in the first game of the world's series of 1923.

This is the way old "Casey" Stengel ran, running his home run home, when two were out in the ninth inning and the score was tied and the ball was still bounding inside the Yankee yard.

This is the way—

His mouth wide open.

His warped old legs bending beneath him at every stride.

His arms flying back and forth like those of a man swimming with a crawl stroke.

His flanks heaving, his breath whistling, his head far back.

URGES HIMSELF ON

Yankee infielders, passed by old "Casey" Stengel as he was running his home run home, say "Casey" was muttering to himself, adjuring himself to greater speed as a jockey mutters to his horse in a race, that he was saying, "Go on, Casey! Go on!"

People generally laugh when they see old "Casey" Stengel run, but they were not laughing when he was running his home run home yesterday afternoon. People—60,000 of them, men and women—were standing in

the Yankee stands and bleachers up there in the Bronx roaring sympa-
thetically, whether they were for or against the Giants.

"Come on, Casey!"

The warped old legs, twisted and bent by many a year of baseball
campaigns, just barely held out under "Casey" Stengel until he reached the
plate, running his home run home.

Then they collapsed.

"CASEY" SLIDES

They gave out just as old "Casey" Stengel slid over the plate in his
awkward fashion with Wally Schang futilely [sic] reaching for him with the
ball. "Billy" Evans, the American League umpire, poised over him in a set
pose, arms spread wide to indicate that old "Casey" was safe.

Half a dozen Giants rushed foward to help "Casey" to his feet, to
hammer him on the back, to bawl congratulations in his ears as he limped
unsteadily, still panting furiously, to the bench where John J. McGraw,
the chief of the Giants, relaxed his stern features to smile for the man who
had won the game.

(NBL)

The police escort an over-competitive Casey from the field. (NBL)

7

CASEY ON ATTITUDE
AND EGO

OR

*"I Couldna
Done It
Without
the Players."*

CASEY STENGEL could certainly lead by example. As his wife Edna somewhat ruefully observed, he was really married to baseball. The couple had no children—unless you count Casey's players—so he was free to pursue baseball 365 days a year.

When everyone else was vacationing, Casey was working. After the Yankees won the 1956 World Series, he was nowhere to be found at the celebration. Someone finally reached him in his hotel room. "I'm just sitting in my room," he said, "trying out a few moves that might help us next year." If this old man, hobbling around on a poorly-set, once-broken leg, was so committed, could any of his players expect less of themselves?

That was Casey's exemplary approach to attitude. His method of dealing with delicate egos was more complicated. At heart Stengel was a player's manager who never forgot the way clubs had exploited him when he was a player. He defended his players in a thousand little ways and went overboard in rewarding over-the-hill players who had been loyal, even tolerating too much drinking. "Drunk again?" Stengel asked pitcher Maury McDermott. "Me too. Good night, Maurice."

But he was also John McGraw's heir, and Little Napoleon's sarcasm and spite survived in his prize pupil. Casey could be unnecessarily brutal, especially to players he felt had showed him up or stolen the limelight from him. But Casey didn't hold grudges against players who held grudges against him. Nor was he as arbitrary and capricious as he sometime seemed; there was often method to his meanness. Understanding his players like the master psychologist he was, Casey knew that nastiness could sometimes be just the tonic some of his men needed.

ATTITUDE

A lazy man is a terrible thing on a ball club. And he may be a man that never breaks a rule. He says, 'I go to bed at eleven o'clock every night.' But he's not awake when he's on the ball field.

"There were things that would irritate Casey Stengel . . . but trying too hard or getting angry at sitting on the bench were not among them."
—MICKEY MANTLE, *The Education of a Baseball Player*

[On Tug McGraw]
He was striking out men with his ambition. He walks on his toes like a girl but he jumps up in the dugout for every out like it was the last out, so you know he's serious about baseball.

Casey and Yogi wait for a relief pitcher.   (UPI/BETTMANN)

"This is the attitude Casey wanted us to cultivate when he urged us to stay loose. He did not mean we should clown it up. He just meant we should stay confident and relaxed, and not allow ourselves to imagine that one strike-out was going to end the season for us."

—MANTLE, *The Education of a Baseball Player*

[To the Yankees in the spring of 1953, after the team had won four straight World Championships]

If we're going to win the pennant, we've got to start thinking we're not as good as we think we are.

Then there's the slipshod man, or I'd-be-better-if-I-had-better-teammates fella. That man, he's got false confidence he's gonna talk his way through the big leagues. Well, he ain't. Here, you gotta work a little harder. I wouldn't play ball just for fun. Find out what you can't do. Come to the park early and eliminate it. Help yourself. That's what bein' in the big leagues means. Can a man hit, run, and slide three ways, and don't let up till the ninth inning is over.

[With the Yankees in Japan]

The name Yankees stands for something all over the world. You players play every game over here as if your job depended on it. It just might.

CONCERN FOR PLAYERS

I couldna done it without the players.

"Casey never held a grudge. He'd pinch-hit for a guy, and the guy would throw his bat. The next day he'd be in the line-up anyway."

—JOHNNY KUCKS

Pittsburgh gave me the same salary Mr. Ebbets had cut me to. I started pretty well in 1918 and went to see the owner, Barney Dreyfuss, about a raise. Hugo Bezdek, the manager, suggested it.

I said, 'Mr. Dreyfuss, do you realize that this is my sixth big-league year but I'm playing for my third-year salary in the big leagues—the salary I got back in 1914? And yet I was traded here as a star. For heaven's sake, I want more money. That was my trouble with the last club.'
He said, 'More money? How do I know you're that good?'
I said, 'I must have been, or you wouldn't have traded for me.'
And he said, 'You didn't do it for me. Show me you're that good this year.'
He always had an answer for everything. If you weren't hitting .300 but doing a lot of other things to help the club, he'd say, 'Wait till you hit .300.' But if you hit over .300, he'd say, 'Your fielding's bad,' or 'You're throwing bad.' Or he'd say, 'Why don't you do some baserunning? Let's do something else. You're just up there hitting for yourself, and you're just up there selfish. Let's get some more of these men around and drive in some more runs.'

"One year Casey was helpful in my contract talks. I seldom got a raise. This time he said, 'If you have any trouble, call me.' I didn't get what I wanted, but I got a pretty good raise. He said, 'How'd you do?' I said, 'All right.' He said, 'Fine.'"
—HANK BAUER

DUREN ON STENGEL

"Casey used to have ongoing feuds with people like Andy Carey, Tony Kubek, and Yogi. Once I saw Yogi swear at Casey in the clubhouse. Casey threw it back, then turned in the opposite direction and winked at someone. It was all water off his back.

"The guys didn't take Casey too seriously. The club was dedicated to winning by example, and there were elder statesmen—players like Mickey Mantle, Bob Turley, and Gil McDougald, and coaches like Frankie Crosetti—to lead. All Casey had to do was handle the guys.

"But he did it very well. He certainly knew how to pump gas in my direction. In Boston he came up to me and said, 'I wanna have dinner with you. I got something serious to talk about.' We just talked—we never talked about anything serious—and he couldn't have been more congenial. I needed that, because I was having some personal problems. I guess that's what the 'serious' talk was all about. Another time he called me into his office at the Stadium and said, 'Sometimes I get busy. You've been doing a hell of a job, and I appreciate it.'

"Sometimes he'd make some really nice gestures. After I'd pitched in the first game of a doubleheader in Washington, he approached me. 'Say, Mr. Duren?'

" 'Yes.'

" 'Where's your glove?'

" 'Under the bench.'

" 'Well, get it. Now take your jacket off and walk slowly to the bullpen. Let the fans see the number on your back. They should get a good look at a star like you.' "

—RYNE DUREN

So what if he [Joe DiMaggio] *doesn't talk to me? I'll get by and so will he. DiMaggio doesn't get paid to talk to me, and I don't either.*

"One thing about Casey, he never hollered at you in front of other people. He needled you, but he didn't holler at you. If he wanted to holler at you, he'd call you in his office."

—YOGI BERRA

"Casey gave me a lot of confidence by telling me I could pitch in any capacity I wanted. I'd been a starter, but I wound up leading the league with 22 saves in 1954. Later he got me into coaching when he said, 'Baseball needs people like you.' He always made me feel ten feet tall. The last time I saw him, he was in the grandstand. He walked up to me and talked as if I was the greatest player in the world.

"We always felt we were going to win under Casey. He treated every game as if it was the biggest we'd ever play. He felt games in spring were as important as games in fall.

"He'd never show you up in front of people. If you were going good, he'd agitate you a little, because he knew you were in a mood to take it. If you were going bad, he'd leave you alone."

—JOHNNY SAIN

"An old Johnny Kucks got a bit of a reprieve in the spring of 1962. Like some of the others there that spring, he didn't stay long enough to appear in the record book. This was the last depot on the track to retirement.

"If Casey had been as heartless and impersonal as some players accused him of being, neither Kucks nor I nor any of the others would have ever had that chance. He gave it to us, and with a chance, who knows, maybe you could win a game or two, even make a living; and if you can make a living doing it, you've got to be pretty good. That was Casey's point . . . .

"Instead of saying, 'We had to better the ball club' or 'This is a trade that will balance the pitching staff'—the kind of thing most managers would say—he only offered his hand and said, 'I know you always did your best: Good luck to you.' Written, it sounds cold; but from the way he said it I know he meant it. It was a sad flight to St. Louis. I never really pitched again."
—KEN MACKENZIE, "Remembering Casey," the *Yale Review*

[To the Mets before their first-ever day of spring training]
You can make a living with this here new club. There ain't nobody got a job won and there ain't nobody can't win one if he shows me he wants to play on my ball club. The owners put a lot of money in here and they want to see how fast you can get better.

"When I came over to the Yankees for the 1954 season, I thought I should be playing every day. Casey took me aside and said, 'Play my way and you'll be around a long time.' He had a great instinct about when I'd hit. He'd use me in right field against righthanders when Bauer was having a hard time, but he also used me in left against some tough lefthanders [Slaughter batted lefthanded] like Billy Pierce and Herb Score. Sometimes he'd pinch-hit me in the first inning! I wound up lasting until I was forty-three, so Casey must have been right."
—ENOS SLAUGHTER

"He was the best manager I ever saw at handling players. You'd expect a lot of moaning and dissension on the Mets, but there wasn't any. Casey made himself the focus.

"He had a great record with pinch-hitters. During the game he'd be thinking out loud on the bench. 'Well, I have Mr. Hodges. I'll use him for the long ball. I have Mr. Ashburn. I'll use him when I need a baserunner.' Guys would think they were the perfect pinch-hitter for some situation or other.

Casey Stengel and Enos Slaughter. (AP/WIDE WORLD PHOTOS)

"Casey used his bench well enough to keep the games close until the late innings. There just wasn't enough talent available to win them." [The 1962 Mets were 19–39 in one-run games.]

—RICHIE ASHBURN

Some men are quiet but ambitious. Some are quiet and don't talk. They won't tell you what their troubles are in playing ball. If you can get a man to talk to you, then you can find out real quick what's wrong with him.

"You played for Casey. Casey took care of everything on top and you took care of things on the field. He liked honesty. In spring training the first year I was with the Mets [1963] he said, 'One thing I appreciate—whether you like me or dislike me—is that if you don't like the way I'm running things come to me and don't go to the press.' He told the whole team this. The day before I got to play for the first time, I said to him, 'I remember what you said in spring training. [I'm] out of sight, out of mind. I'm twenty-one years old. I'm not a bullpen catcher. I'd like to play here. If I can't, why don't you send me someplace where I can play. At least I'll be ready when you need me.'

" 'You want to play that bad?' he said.

" 'Yeah.'

" 'O.K., you'll play tomorrow.'

"We went to Cincinnati and I played my first game against Jim Maloney, Joe Nuxhall and the Reds. I went 4-for-4. The next day, Casey said he knew that Cincinnati was not a major-league town: 'They can't even put 1.000 on the scoreboard when a kid is batting 1.000.' That made me feel good. You just loved Casey. He loved hustle and he hated anyone dogging it."

—RON HUNT

"Before the 1950 World Series Casey announced, 'Reynolds will pitch against Robin Roberts.' That didn't hurt Vic Raschi's feelings because it's always an honor to pitch the opener [Raschi started it against the Phils' Jim Konstanty]. Casey was giving both of us confidence.

"Casey always said about me, 'He can handle the good teams.' He always talked about oil with me, because I'm from Oklahoma. He owned some oil wells, but the talk was really a way to get my attention: talking about me and where I was from.

"In the 1951 Series, with Mays up and men on base, Casey came out and said, 'Did you ever throw a curve to this fella?'

" 'No, I never have.'

" 'Don't you think this might be a good time to try it?'

" 'Sure.'

Casey started walking away. Then he turned around and said, 'Oh, by the way, keep it down.' Of course, a curve has to be down to be effective.

"I did throw it down, and Mays hit into a double play. I looked over to Casey, and he had his thumb and index finger in a circle: 'O.K.' "

—ALLIE REYNOLDS

125

Before the 1934 season, New York Giants manager Bill Terry said of the Dodgers, "Are they still in the league?" Casey's Dodgers got revenge by costing the Giants the pennant with a sweep at the Polo Grounds on the last weekend of the season. The Cardinals, meanwhile, won the league championship.

A SEASON ENDS

" 'In the tenth inning with everything lost they booed me [said Terry]. I thought I was in St. Louis.'

"You felt sorry for him. You excused his bitterness.

"Someone mentioned Brooklyn. Bill's eyes mirrored his anger as he said, 'If Stengel's team had played as hard all year as it did the last two days, it would not be in sixth place.'

"Terry was asked if he would go to Detroit [for the World Series].

" 'Nope,' he said. 'It would be too humiliating.'

"In the Dodger clubhouse the din was deafening. Casey Stengel, clad in a bath towel draped diaper-fashion about his hips, was delivering the general's farewell to his troops. His voice was hoarse from its duties in the coaching box. His arms thrashed wildly.

" 'Farewell, my bonny men. Some of you are off to maim the gentle rabbit. Some of you will shoot the carefree deer. I bid you Godspeed, my lambie-pies, my brave young soldiers. Go with Casey's blessing upon your sweet heads.'

"Someone interrupted to report Terry's remarks. Stengel grinned. 'So he feels bad, eh? How do you think I felt when he made fun of my ball club last spring?'

"Casey hooked his finger into the air in the fashion of Demosthenes delivering a phillipic. 'So he says if we had played hard we wouldn't finish in sixth place? Well, if the season lasted another month and we'd kept playing him he'd finish in last place!'

"The Dodgers cheered to the echo.

"Casey continued: 'He's feeling bad, eh? Well, I'm feeling bad, too. I didn't get any World Series pay check, either. I wish I had his money. They could boo the ears off me. You've got to learn to take it in this business.'

"Casey held up his hand for attention.

" 'Just a minute, gentlemen of the press,' he said. 'Those were Brooklyn fans who did the booing. There isn't a finer, sweeter, better gentleman or lady on God's green footstool than a Brooklyn fan. Three cheers for the Brooklyn fans, my hearties, and'—he turned to glower savagely—'the first mug that doesn't cheer gets a kick in the shins.' The entire company cheered."

—JIMMY POWERS, *New York Daily News*

[To his players, on the subject of personal appearances]
Make 'em pay you a thousand dollars. Don't go help those people with their shows for coffee-and-cake money. You're the Yankees—the best. Make 'em pay you high.

SMITH ON STENGEL

"At no previous time in the [1950 World] Series had [the Phillies] seemed so immature and futile, so hopelessly beyond their depth in a man's game, as they did against the blond boy graduate of the Yankees' Kansas City prep school. He [Whitey Ford] had them shut out, 5 to 0, and the World Series was over when Gene Woodling, playing left field, botched up a fly ball and let two Philadelphia runs come home.

"Casey Stengel is a wise old gent. Back in the World Series of 1941, when Hugh Casey was beating the Yankees for the Dodgers until his catcher, Mickey Owen, failed to catch the strike that should have ended the game, a crazy panic swept Ebbets Field. In the shrieking excitement, nobody had the sense to go out and remind the pitcher that he still had the game won, that there were two out and a runner on first base and all he had to do was retire one more batter. Everybody went frantic that day, and in the confusion the Yankees made off with the ballgame.

"Now, before the crowd was through shouting about Woodling's error, Stengel was out on the mound telling Ford the score. It was still 5 to 2, Casey said, with one man on base. Casey just stood there in the middle of the hubbub talking quietly to the kid, patting him briskly on the rear of his lap until Bill McGowan, the umpire, moved in from his station at second base to break up the kaffeeklatsch.

"Maybe Ford was upset in spite of Casey. Or maybe he was tired. Or perhaps Mike Goliat was due to get a hit then. Anyhow, Goliat did hit, and Casey walked out again and patted Ford's stern some more and prodded

127

his bosom with a gnarled finger and talked some more. But now he was apologizing to the kid for what he had to do. He had announced his decision and two umpires, Charles Berry and Jocko Conlan, were signaling the bullpen to send in a righthander.

"Allie Reynolds came striding in, lugging his glove and a windbreaker, and Ford walked to the dugout, pulled on a jacket, got a long drink at the watercooler, and stayed to watch the finish.

"Know what Casey had said to Ford when the manager took him out? Casey said: 'There's a stinkin' little ground ball between third and shortstop and it's my fault. I should have had Rizzuto over there, but he didn't see me waving at him.'

"That was a lie, of course, from a very considerate liar."

—RED SMITH

CASEY AS TASKMASTER

"Stengel liked Phil Rizzuto a lot more than Rizzuto liked Stengel. The little shortstop had given him the best year of his life, 1950, when he was the American League MVP. But by 1956 Rizzuto was only a spare part, and an expendable one at that. In those days, the Yankees could afford to look weeks ahead to the World Series, and Stengel decided he needed a left-handed hitting outfielder to do battle against the National League–leading Dodgers. The one they wanted was Enos Slaughter, and they had to activate him before September 1 to make him eligible for the Series roster. Which meant that somebody else had to go.

"Rizzuto was called into Stengel's office, and, he said, 'I couldn't imagine what he wanted.' General Manager George Weiss was there, too, and the two men told Rizzuto about the chance to get Slaughter and the problem they faced. They asked Rizzuto to look over the roster and suggest who might be dropped. Rizzuto naively offered up the names of a spare catcher and a spare pitcher, and Stengel patiently explained why he needed those men. Then it dawned on Rizzuto, and before Weiss could explain that they would keep him on salary and restore him to the roster after September 1, Phil was out the door. He took off his uniform, got dressed, and left the stadium. His playing career was over."

—DANIEL OKRENT AND STEVE WULF, *Baseball Anecdotes*

[To outfielder Bob Cerv]
Nobody knows this, but one of us has just been traded to Kansas City.

[When Brooklyn pitcher Boom-Boom Beck kicked a water cooler]

Stop that. If you break a toe I won't be able to get anything for you.

"He always used me as a scapegoat. He would chew my ass out when he wanted to get on some other guys. He knew that when he could get me mad I was a more aggressive and better ballplayer. In fact, he had that in a book he wrote: 'Make him mad.'"

—ANDY CAREY

Phil "The Scooter" Rizutto. (AP/WIDE WORLD PHOTOS)

CASEY [Going to the mound]: Stallard's ready. I'm putting him in.
PITCHER ALVIN JACKSON: I'm not tired.
CASEY: He's not tired either.

[On Jerry Lumpe's prowess in batting practice]
He looks like the greatest hitter in the world until you play him.

MACKENZIE ON STENGEL

"[Jimmy] Piersall hit a home run one day in the Polo Grounds, and as it turned out—although none of us knew it at the time—it was the hundredth of his career. When he got to first base and turned toward second, he pivoted completely around and ran the rest of the way backwards. The fans loved it. Warren Giles, president of the National League, did not. Three days later Piersall had a telegram from him.

"We were having one of our 'pre-series' clubhouse meetings—Solly Hemus presiding—on the day the telegram arrived. Normally Casey didn't bother to attend, but this day he just happened to be there. When everyone had assembled, Piersall hauled out the telegram and read it for all to hear. It went something like this: 'The League office takes exception to your performance on Tuesday last, and in the future any such performance will force us to take disciplinary action against you. Signed, Warren Giles.' He folded up the telegram and announced: 'Well, when I hit my two hundredth I'm going to slide at every fuckin' base. I guess there's no fuckin' rule against that. HA, HA, HA, HA.' At this point Casey got up from his chair and walked over in front of Piersall. Everybody wondered what was coming next. Casey bent over as though he were going to say something in confidence to him but then for everyone to hear he said, 'And I guess if they throw you a good curve with two strikes there's no rule that says you can't swing, either. HA, HA, HA, HA.' The same cynical laugh that Jimmy had used. It was very clear to everyone that there was room for only one clown and one ringmaster in this circus, and it was going to be Casey. Two days later Piersall was gone."
—KEN MacKENZIE, *Remembering Casey* [In fact, Piersall wasn't released until a month later. He was batting .194.]

"You open the paper in the morning and read how lousy you are."
— CLETE BOYER

"Shake my hand? He wasn't even there to say good-bye."
— JOE PAGE, on his retirement

"One of the few rules Casey put down for his [Mets] players was that there would be no card playing. It was his belief that card playing led to gambling, gambling led to losing, and losing led to resentments. Shortly after Harry Chiti was obtained by the Mets, he went to Stengel during an airplane trip and asked for permission to start a gin-rummy game. Stengel said no. He suggested instead that if Chiti, a catcher, had nothing to do he might go over the opposition hitters. Chiti went to sleep."
— LEONARD SCHECTER

"Casey was a great psychologist. He slapped Allie Reynolds on the back every time he pitched, but he never said five words to Vic Raschi and he might have patted me on the shoulder one time. Vic and I discussed it every now and then. We never did figure out why he did what he did. But it didn't matter: We knew when we did a good or bad job.

"We were in Detroit one time for a doubleheader. We played real sloppy the first time, making all kinds of mental errors. The second game starts, and in the fifth inning we're leading 14–2 and he's raising all kinds of hell on the bench. 'This guy did this' and 'That guy did that.'

"We asked him one time on a train about the Detroit incident. He started laughing. 'I know that I got a bunch of players who know how to play. I don't have to tell them how to do this or how to do that. When they do bad, I know that they're mad. If I try to tell them something at that time, I'm liable to get a punch right in the mouth. When you're winning, you can call that player anything and he'll accept it and retain it more than he will the other way.' "
— EDDIE LOPAT

"[Mets owner] Joan Payson used to take the players over to West Palm Beach for a big dinner. Everyone was eating steaks and drinking Lancer's wine and getting into a pretty good mood. Stengel was up at the microphone talking about taking care of your money and putting it into annuities. If anyone knew how sound he was about money, they would have been listening. He had some other advice:

" 'Guys, when you're going out after the game, don't go out with five or six

other guys. By the time everyone buys back, you're drunk. Go out in smaller groups.'

"Duke Carmel, who was sure he was going to make the team, had been drinking some wine. He chimed in, 'I saw you out the other day with ten guys.' That was true, but it wasn't something you should say with Casey up at the microphone. Suddenly the air conditioner came on—whoooo—and the place quieted down. 'I seen you too when you didn't see me,' Casey said to Carmel. 'And I'll tell you another thing—you haven't made this club yet.' The next day Duke Carmel's locker was empty. Casey was tough."

—RON SWOBODA

"[Tommy Henrich] put on all his speed, and just as he reached for the ball he crashed into the wall. The pain was crushing. He lay in the outfield knowing that it was a serious injury. Casey Stengel rushed out to right field and hovered over him like a mother hen. 'Lie down,' he commanded. 'Don't get up, take it very easy.' He really cares about me, Henrich thought through the gasps of pain, that coldness that I felt in the past wasn't real. This man cares. I was wrong. 'Lie down and give me a little more time to get someone warmed up and get this clown out of here,' Stengel added."

—DAVID HALBERSTAM, Summer of '49

"His egotism, so immense, was really concentrated on the teaching function. He wanted to mold, to create. His pride was attached not to mere winning, but to winning through his instruction and leadership. He didn't want to be hailed for the sensational statistics the Yankees compiled, but for the fact that they were compiled by men he chose and guided.

"There were two principal roots of this desire. The first was frustrated fatherhood: having no children of his own, Stengel made many a young ball player into a surrogate son. The results were remarkably true to life—not all sons are comfortable with their fathers, especially when the fathers drive them toward an achievement the father chose; and not all fathers understand the best way to handle their sons. And, as happens so often, it is only when the son is older and more mature that he comes to appreciate what the old man did, or tried to do, for him. It was common to hear players (Hank Bauer and Gene Woodling became prime examples) who chafed under Stengel's authority and hated him passionately, admit afterward that they had better records and longer careers because of Stengel's handling."

—LEONARD KOPPETT, A Thinking Man's Guide to Baseball

(UPI/BETTMANN)

"He knew who to get mad at and who to leave alone. I was playing right field against righthanded pitchers, but he left me out of an entire series against righthanders in Detroit, where I always hit well. What he was doing was getting me ready and stirring me up for the Cleveland series. When we got there, I hit like hell. He'd do the same stuff with Bauer. Remember, Hank and I were two squareheads. I was mad at the time, but I thank Casey now."

—GENE WOODLING

"The first time I heard Casey speak was in spring training of '49. If I knew he was going to use a platoon system, my impression would have been horseshit of

133

him. But those days you were through at thirty-five or thirty-six. I platooned with Gene Woodling for a while, and I played until I was thirty-nine and Gene until he was forty. I told Gene maybe Casey prolonged our careers. Gene said, 'You might be right.' You can't bitch when he takes you to the bank every year."

—HANK BAUER

CASEY AND THE ASS

"It was 1973, the second year that the Oakland A's were in the World Series, and this time they were playing the Mets. Stengel, as usual, went to the Series. I remember him standing in line at the registration desk of the Edgewater Hyatt Hotel in Oakland and wearing a little porkpie Mets hat with the brim turned up. Now, the mascot of the A's, that burro named Charlie O., pretty much had the run of the hotel. Even though there was a corral for him in the patio, management let him out and he roamed around the lobby.

"Stengel had proceeded to the registration desk and was signing in when the burro came by and butted him in the back with his head.

"Casey hardly seemed to notice and continued signing in. Then the burro whammed him again. This time Casey turned around and gave a double- and triple-take.

"He looked at Si Burick, of the Dayton Daily News, who was standing nearby, and raised his eyebrows. 'That's some horse, that horse,' said Stengel. 'I haven't been here in a year and he recognizes me.' "

—TOM CALLAHAN

8

CASEY ON RACE

OR

*"Give Me
an All-Star Team
of Them and Let
Me Manage."*

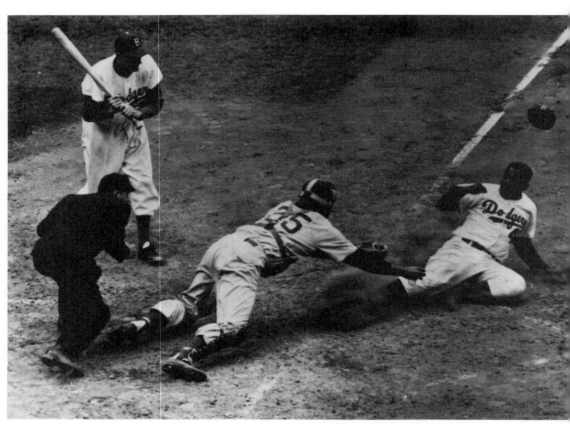

Jackie Robinson steals home against the Chicago Cubs in 1952. (UPI/BETTMANN)

CASEY WAS FIFTY-SIX years old when Jackie Robinson made his major-league debut in 1947, and he carried the racial baggage of many whites born in the nineteenth century. He used all the vicious code words about blacks, and his reluctance to integrate the Yankees until 1955—reinforced by team executives George Weiss, Del Webb, and Dan Topping—probably weakened the entire American League.

But any glib generalization about Casey's racial attitudes clashes with his actual treatment of black players. Even in his early days, long before integration, he was helping them. He was a great supporter of Elston Howard, who integrated Stengel's Yankees, and in turn Howard defended Casey to the end. Al Jackson, the former Met and current pitching coach of the Orioles, was another of Casey's favorites. Whatever Casey's attitudes may have been, he was a pragmatist who knew black athletes would help him if he reciprocated. His actions usually spoke louder—and prouder—than his words.

CASEY AND THE BULLET

"No one knows how great the Bullet [Bullet Joe Rogan, a pitcher in the Negro leagues] had been in his peak years in his twenties. He was already thirty, toiling in obscurity for an army team under a boiling Arizona sun in 1919, when he was discovered by a former Kansas City dental student named Charles D. ['KC'] Stengel, then an outfielder with the Pittsburgh Pirates barnstorming through the Southwest. Casey recalled:

" 'I first saw Rogan down below Albuquerque. We were down near the Mexican border, and the Army brought these buglers, and made all the soldiers line up and march across the ball field like this and pick up pebbles and rocks so we could play.

" 'We had a big guy for St. Paul in the American Association who cheated. So before the game I went out behind home plate and announced:

" '[Stentorian voice] "Ladies and gentlemen"—but there were no ladies there—"ladies and gentlemen, we're now going to have a young man that pitches this game today that throws that new, mysterious ball known as the *Tequila Pitch!* It's taken from the tequila plant." And Jesus, he was spitting all over the ball and everything else, you know, and cheating. So we won the game.'

"But Casey was impressed with the stocky black doughboy with the jug handle curve. 'You know how Rogan pitched, don't you?' Stengel asked. 'He pitched like this: without a windup. If you lean in, see, he pitches close; if you step back, you know what he'd come with? Outside.'

"When Casey got back home to Kansas City that winter, he looked up J.L. Wilkinson, a white man who was forming a new club called the Monarchs, and told him about Rogan and half a dozen other black soldier stars. Bullet Joe's career was launched at the age of thirty."

—JOHN B. HOLWAY, *Black Ball Stars*

Has anybody ever told you about Dobie Moore [another black star Stengel encountered in Arizona]? *Well, I'll tell you something about him. That Moore was one of the best shortstops that will ever live! That fella could stand up to the plate and hit right-handed, he could hit line drives out there just as far as you want to see.*

"Sitting so close, I could also hear the racist remarks coming from the opposing dugout that were directed at my father, Jackie Robinson, and the other black Dodgers. Eddie Stanky, when he managed the Cardinals, was particularly abusive and encouraged his players to emulate him. Casey Stengel is so beloved that it may surprise some people that he was particularly insulting to blacks; he was a racist who used the word 'nigger' as if he thought it were appropriate."

—ROY CAMPANELLA, JR.

[On Elston Howard]
Well, they finally get me a nigger, I get the only one who can't run.

"Throughout his minor league career Howard had played the outfield. Upon his arrival in Florida, Manager Casey Stengel informed him that he would be converted

into a catcher. 'As an outfielder he would never be more than a minor leaguer,' commented Stengel. 'In order to play up here, he'd best turn his efforts to catching.' To many observers, the position switch constituted another ploy by the Yankees to avoid integration. . . .

"Yet whatever the Yankees' past sins, the allegations regarding the treatment of Howard in 1954 appear unjustified. Howard's minor league record did not merit promotion and although the durable Berra remained the regular Yankee catcher for several more years, the transfer of Howard from the outfield proved beneficial to both him and the Yankees. The following spring after a banner season at Kansas City, Howard joined the New York club with whom he played or coached for all but two seasons until his death in 1980."

—JULES TYGIEL, *Baseball's Great Experiment*

[After the part-Cree Allie Reynolds struck out Jackie Robinson three times in a 1952 Series game]

Before that black son-of-a-bitch accuses us of being prejudiced, he should learn how to hit an Indian.

"[Howard] Cosell was a neighbor and close friend of Jackie Robinson. Robinson never attended a Mets game but was kept abreast of the Stengel doings by Cosell. Robinson was happy to hear negative things about Casey sleeping on the bench or maligning black players or drinking heavily. The animosity went back as far as 1949 when Stengel joined the Yankees, and Robinson was with Brooklyn. Stengel often used the term 'nigger' for black players in those days and went even further [by] calling blacks 'coons' or 'jungle bunnies,' terms of derision often used only by the worst of bigots. Stengel was born in Kansas City in 1890. Few people born in Kansas City in 1890 did not use those terms, and, unfortunately, it was not until too many years later that Stengel decided to stop using them."

—MAURY ALLEN, *Jackie Robinson: A Life Remembered*

"I never felt any prejudice around Casey. He'd scream at Newcombe and Robinson and Campanella during the World Series, but I never heard him scream racial things. He screamed at Reese and Hodges and Snider, too. . . .

"He always bragged about me, called me his three-way platoon [Howard caught, played the outfield, and could play first base], and treated me with kindness and respect. I never saw any signs of bigotry. . . .

"In Kansas City and Chicago they wouldn't serve me in the restaurants until

Stengel raised hell. Stengel told the hotel, 'We came as a ball club and Elston Howard is part of the ball club. If he can't be accommodated, we'll leave.' "

—ELSTON HOWARD

"He never treated me with anything but respect. . . .

"He gave me a chance when the Pittsburgh Pirates didn't. When I beat Bob Gibson and the Cards 1–0 on the last weekend of the tight 1964 pennant race, Casey bragged about it for a long, long time."

—ALVIN JACKSON

Now when I broke into baseball years and years ago we used to have Irish and German and Polish players. And then the greatest players came from the South. Then they came from Texas, and then they came from Chicago.
Today [1962] *it's the colored player. He's a good runner, and he's very quick with his wrists. He's the best hitter. The Italians are the second best hitters. The Polish player is sometimes slow and sluggish swinging the bat. The Germans are passing out, the race has gotten mixed up so much, and it's the same with the Irish. They don't talk and act like the ones that had just come from Ireland.* [Stengel himself was half Irish and half German.]

"He was a racist only in the casual, unthinking way that most of his generation of Americans were. Racial and ethnic slurs were characteristic of his era—you called a Swede a squarehead, a Frenchman a frog, an Italian a wop, a Jew a kike, an Irishman a mick, a Spaniard a spic, and so on—and his own sarcastic, parodying nature jumped on a man's obvious features: flop ears, big nose, black skin. . . .

"When Jim Brown, the famous Cleveland Browns running back, was dominating professional football, someone asked Stengel if he thought Brown would make a good baseball player. 'Why wouldn't he?' Stengel demanded. 'He's big and strong and a good athlete. If he's good in one sport, why wouldn't he be good in another? I tell ya, I'd like to sign that big, black—' He stopped abruptly, his racial sensitivities obviously heightened since [Elston] Howard's rookie days. Some of the people with him laughed. 'Well, I'd like to try it,' Stengel went on defensively. 'I bet he could play. Goddammit, there may be too many of them but give me an All-Star team of them and let me manage.' "

—ROBERT W. CREAMER, *Stengel*

9

Casey's Favorite Players

Stengel published the list on the following page in his autobiography, *Casey at the Bat*. There weren't many surprises on it because Casey knew a Hall-of-Famer when he saw one. However, note the loyalty to ex-Yankees and the underrated Glenn Wright. Also note that Sandy Koufax wasn't listed, because he didn't have his best years until after 1960.

Following are some comments on Stengel's all-stars and other favorites.

1912–60
CATCHER

He [Yogi Berra] *knew all the hitters better'n anybody else, and he knew his own pitchers as well as the ones he hit against.*
He could go out and wake the pitcher up when the fella wasn't throwing the way he should be, even if he thought he was. . . .
That fella only hits when he sees a dollar sign. Wait till September 20. Then watch him hit. . . .
For years they been askin' me, 'Why do you ketch this poor boy every day? Why do you ketch him doubleheaders when it's a hundred in the shade? You want to burn the poor boy out?' Did I wear him out? He's still here, ain't he? The only man that was here when I come to New York in '49.
Still, where would I be or where would he be if he wasn't here ketchin' all those games, or the owners, too? He looks like a bear, and he can swing that bat and he can get out across the plate for a bunt farther than anybody and he knows what's going on in the office besides. He can get along with the pitchers. If I'd been ketchin' here for twelve years I'd of had forty riots with pitchers, but he slaps 'em across the behind

CASEY'S ALL-STAR TEAM
(1912–60)

	NATIONAL LEAGUE	AMERICAN LEAGUE
1B	Bill Terry Johnny Mize	Lou Gehrig George Sisler
2B	Rogers Hornsby Jackie Robinson	Eddie Collins Charlie Gehringer Napoleon Lajoie
SS	Honus Wagner Ernie Banks Glenn Wright	Joe Cronin Luke Appling Phil Rizzuto
3B	Frankie Frisch Pie Traynor	Buck Weaver
LF	Stan Musial Zack Wheat	Ted Williams
CF	Willie Mays Edd Roush Duke Snider	Ty Cobb Joe DiMaggio Tris Speaker
RF	Paul Waner	Babe Ruth Joe Jackson
C	Gabby Hartnett Roy Campanella Ernie Lombardi	Mickey Cochrane Bill Dickey Yogi Berra
P	Grover Alexander Christy Mathewson Carl Hubbell Dizzy Dean Warren Spahn Ed Reulbach Dazzy Vance	Walter Johnson Bob Feller Lefty Grove Ed Walsh Allie Reynolds Vic Raschi Chief Bender

and says, 'Don't worry, I ain't gonna call for nothin'
different. . . .'
Maybe he can't say it good, but he can do it.

"*Stengel seldom refers to his players by name. This is a distinction he denies all but his stars, the top columnists, and a select few among 'his' writers. In discussing his team, he will refer to 'the third baseman's arm, or the speed of 'my leftfielder,' and only those listeners familiar with the makeup of the team will be able to follow him accurately. So high has Berra risen in his estimation that Casey often refers to him slyly as 'Mr. Berra.' "*

—FRANK GRAHAM, *Casey Stengel*

He [Al Lopez] *was a terrific man for the pitchers, because he could catch those low pitches and make them look good to the umpires.*

Campanella . . . was a slick catcher. He looked like he had a fat stomach, but that stomach didn't bother him at all. He was a nimble man. And he was a splendid lowball catcher—he could squat behind home plate with his fanny actually touching the ground.
Another thing about Campanella was the fact that he had a very good disposition. He came up when we first commenced having Negroes in the big league, and I think he got by with as little trouble, for being a catcher, as anybody possibly could. When you're catching you can get in trouble no matter what your color is, because you've got to block a runner off from home plate, and he's got to knock you down when he runs in.

FIRST BASE

[On Johnny Mize]
A slugger who hit like a leadoff man.

"*When Johnny Mize joined the Yankees, he cut down his power swing to a contact swing. This is the kind of player Casey liked: a guy who could do anything necessary to get the job done.*"

—JOHNNY SAIN

[On Gil Hodges]

He fields better on one leg than anybody else I got on two.

[On Lou Gehrig]

They sometimes wondered if he wasn't as good as Ruth, or better than Ruth.

SECOND BASE

[On Eddie Collins]

He could field, he could run bases, he could steal signs. He could hit any kind of pitching, he could place the ball anywhere you wanted it.

[On Jackie Robinson]

All you guys, when you get into the locker room I want you to check your lockers. He stole everything out there he wanted today so he might have stolen your jocks as well.

[On Billy Martin]

What about Martin, what if he didn't catch Robinson's pop-up in the World Series, who was gonna catch it, 'cause the wind was blowing and a lot of people stood around waiting for it to stop blowing, but he went and got it for the out, and three runs were coming around the bases, so he's not such a bad fellow like they make him out if he can do that for you.

"Billy was usually in trouble on the field, fighting the other team with his mouth and his fists, as well as with bat and glove. One day he and Jim Piersall of the Red Sox rolled in the dirt, punching and mauling each other. Stengel, who never restricted Billy's use of his tongue, did not like to see him risk banishment from a game because of a fight. "If I'd wanted a fighter," he told Martin, "I would have hired Rocky Marciano."

—FRANK GRAHAM, *Casey Stengel*

THIRD BASE

[On Frankie Frisch]

I haf-ta say Mr. Frisch treated me handsome. He told me to play deep and that he'd come back and catch the short ones and I haf-ta say he did. The man was so fast and so quick going to his left that he could play a deep second base and not only come back to center field, but he also could run diagonal down toward the right-field line and catch short flies near the fence. . . .

But I'd rather have him at third base on this team. . . . Frisch was so fast that he could dive for balls and head them off, and then get up and throw the man out. He really had it all—in the field, on the bases, and up at the plate, where he hit both righthanded and lefthanded. And he was very aggressive.

[On Billy Cox]

"I remember being at a spring training game in Miami in 1964. The Mets were playing the Orioles, and before the game Met manager Casey Stengel was holding forth in the dugout. Brooks Robinson came strolling by to get a bat and got up to take some batting practice. Casey yelled out, 'You are the second-greatest third baseman who ever lived.'

"Brooks stopped in his tracks and walked over to the dugout. 'Who's the best?' he asked.

"Casey said quickly, 'Number 3. Used to play in Brooklyn. He had a better arm than you, Brooksie, a better arm. There was nobody like him. But don't feel badly. You're the second-best and he was in a world all his own.' "

—LARRY KING

SHORTSTOP

[On Honus Wagner]

" 'It's a funny thing about ballplayers,' [Casey Stengel] mused. 'Folks go around picking top players in every position and they say: "He was great, but . . ." Then they'd mention some weakness. However, no one could ever say any "buts" about old Honus. It had to be, "He was great. Period." He had no weakness and could do everything superlatively well. I know that John McGraw said the Dutchman was a greater player than Ty Cobb or Babe Ruth. Ed Barrow said the same thing. Sometimes I wonder if they ain't right.' "

—ARTHUR DALEY

He [a Brooklyn pitcher named Wheezer Dell] *would get on the mound, get into a jam, and all of a sudden you would start hearin' this whoop, whoop, this wheezin' you know, which is why they wuz callin' him Wheezer then and now. This one time Wagner was the hitter and he complained to the umpire he couldn't concentrate on the ball what with Wheezer giving him that 'whoops, whoops' from his wheezin', and damned if the umpire didn't go to the mound and tell him to quit it. Wheezer said he couldn't help it and the umpire asked him not to do it on this one hitter, Wagner, because he was a big star and he didn't want to hold up the game none. Wheezer held his breath and pitched and Wagner hit it off the wall. He commenced wheezin' in the shower after that.*

[On Phil Rizzuto]
If I were a retired gentleman, I would follow the Yankees around just to see Rizzuto work those miracles every day. . . .
What about the shortstop Rizzuto who got nothing but daughters but throws out the lefthanded hitters in the double play? . . .
Rizzuto is the greatest shortstop I ever saw. He can't hit with Honus Wagner, but I've seen him make plays that the old Dutchman couldn't. . . .

[On Harvey Kuenn]
If the guy was hurt, his team might be hurt, but the pitching all over the league will improve.

PITCHER

[On Whitey Ford]
He was my banty rooster. Whitey used to stick out his chest, like this, and walk out on the mound against any of those big pitchers. They talk about the fall of the Yankees. Well, the Yankees would have fallen a lot sooner if it wasn't for my banty rooster.

[On Vic Raschi]

"It was the whole works the next day and the realization for Stengel that he was on the brink of a major league pennant. He went to Vic Raschi for the big one and the big, bear-like righthander came through for him. Years later Casey was to single out Raschi as the best pitcher he ever had with the Yankees. Why?

" 'Because,' said Stengel, 'he had it here, here and here.' Casey touched first his arm, then his head and then finally placed his hand over his heart."

—HAROLD ROSENTHAL

[On Grover Cleveland Alexander]

Every ball that he threw would break—even his fastball.

[On Warren Spahn]

He can hold runners on first. Then they don't often go from first to third on you, and you get more forceouts at second and more double plays.

OUTFIELD

[On Enos Slaughter]

He broke a shoulder for me once, trying to make a catch. You can still see the scar where they operated on him. He will slide for you and dive for a low hit ball and hit the ground and he will hit the wall for you if he has to. Slaughter was brought up right.

[On Ted Williams]

And that fella . . . is only the greatest lefthanded hitter I saw in both leagues in the last twenty years. He had the best judgment of a strike of any man in the game, and he's well over six feet, which gives him a bigger strike zone than most hitters, and he could still judge a pitch better than the umpires who were seeing the ball from straight on while he was up there standing sideways.

"Casey felt that the great outfielders played so shallow they were like extra shortstops. That's why he liked Tris Speaker and would have liked Paul Blair. Today fielders stand in front of the wall and rarely catch a humpbacked liner.

"He thought DiMaggio was the best all-around player he'd ever seen. He liked

the way Joe could go from first to third without being thrown out or from second to home without sliding. He also liked how Joe caught everything at chest level in center field, because he knew the pitching.

"He thought Tommy Henrich was smart, knowledgeable about pitchers and strike zones, and could handle the bat and make quick decisions. Tommy was especially good at setting up pitchers. In the 1949 World Series Don Newcombe got him out several times on high pitches. Then Tommy hit a high one out to beat him 1–0. In the earlier at bats he'd just been looking at Newc's stuff.

"Casey liked late-inning guys like Babe Herman, who could deliver in a big spot. Ty Cobb was the only player of his time who could actually put backspin on bunts. Casey liked subtle things like that."

—MAURY ALLEN

[On Tommy Henrich]
He's a fine judge of a fly ball. He fields grounders like an infielder. He never makes a wrong throw, and if he comes back to the hotel at three in the morning when we're on the road and says he's been sitting up with a sick friend, he's been sitting up with a sick friend.

[On Joe DiMaggio]
The best thing he had—and I'll give you a tip—was his head. He saw some of the faults of the pitcher and he would hit the ball, and he didn't just hit it on Sunday, neither . . . . DiMaggio could hit a ball off the moon.

[On Stan Musial]
We're playin' the Cardinals and they got this kid, just up from the minors at the end of the year. I know all about his record and how he's supposed to be great and a lefthanded hitter and all. But he's a kid. And I know how it is with kids, they can all hit fastballs, but they can't hit the soft stuff, because they've just come from the minors and who's down there that's a good experienced pitcher and knows how to mix it up, right? So he's been lookin' at fastballs and wild men and now I tell my pitcher, don't worry about it, just give him those little soft curves and he'll break his back swingin' at it—and he hit two singles and two doubles off my pitcher, and that's when I found out this Mr. Musial was a

pretty good hitter whether he was young and had seen old pitching or not.

[On Zack Wheat]
He was the most graceful lefthanded hitter I ever saw. With the dead ball, many of his line drives were caught, but they were just shot out of a cannon almost every time up.

[On Paul Waner]
For a little man, he was the greatest hitter I ever saw—I didn't see Willie Keeler play. Waner could hit the ball to all fields, and he was a good little fielder in the outfield.

[On Bob Meusel]
Bob Meusel was a big tall man but amazingly nimble. One of the best baserunners, if he decided to run. He was a fellow that if he could put it all out, he had it some days better than anybody. He was the most amazing thrower I ever saw in my life. He could stand flat-footed in the outfield and throw to home plate. That's the kind of arm he had.
In the 1923 World Series, I hit a ball right near the bullpen, and as I was circling the bases Whitey Whitt picked up the ball and flipped it to Meusel. With that tremendous arm of his he cut the ball loose and it came clear into home plate and it was just four inches off or I'da been out at home plate. It was one of the most tremendous throws ever made.

[On Babe Ruth]
Now this fellow in Atlanta [Hank Aaron] *is amazing. He hits the ball the best for a man of his size. But I can't say he hits the ball better than Ruth. Ruth could hit the ball so far nobody could field it . . . .*
I chased the balls that Babe Ruth hit . . . .
He was very brave at the plate. You rarely saw him fall away from a pitch. He stayed right in there. No one drove him out.

[On Ty Cobb]
I never saw anyone like Cobb. No one even close to him.

(NBL)

151

When he wiggled those wild eyes at a pitcher, you knew you were looking at the one bird nobody could beat. It was like he was superhuman.

JACKS-OF-ALL-TRADES

[On Johnny Cooney]

"He liked Johnny Cooney, who could handle the bat, hit down on the ball, always get a piece of it, and rarely strike out."

—AL LOPEZ

The best ballplayer's the one who doesn't think he'd made good. He keeps trying to convince you. That's what keeps a fella like Cooney going; the guy still doesn't believe he's come through after all these years.

1960–75

[On Willie Mays]

I was out to Dodger Stadium and saw that man . . . who they say is getting old and all he did was make three assists against the fastest running team in baseball. He still charges the ball better than any of 'em and that old arm throws out a lot of young legs.
Mays catches fifty balls a year that the others don't get. That park he plays in [Candlestick] has wind blowing which gives the other fellas fits but Willie can catch a ball in a windstorm.

[On Roger Maris]

I give him one point for speed. I do this because he can run fast. I give him another point because he can slide fast. Then I give him a point because he can bunt. I also give him a point because he can field, very good around the fences, even on top of the fences. Next, I give him a point because he can throw . . . . So I add up my points and I've got five for him even before I come to his hitting. I would say this is a good man.

[On Sandy Koufax]

"Casey Stengel once said that Sandy was probably the best pitcher who ever lived.

He said, 'Forget the other fellow,' meaning Walter Johnson. 'You can forget Waddell. The Jewish kid is probably the best of them all.' "

—ED ROEBUCK

"Casey loved Hot Rod Kanehl. He was a guy who never made it until the '62 Mets, when he was twenty-eight years old. He kept grinding it out without a whole lot of ability but with a lot of desire. He could play seven different positions and get himself hit by a pitch with the bases loaded."

—RICHIE ASHBURN

1975—(PLAYERS CASEY WOULD HAVE LIKED)

"Casey would have liked Robin Yount and Paul Molitor—all-around professionals who can play a couple of positions and hang in good. He'd like the Giants' Matt Williams, who moved from third to short in the World Series. And he'd like the kid in Chicago who was named after me: Ryne Sandberg." [That's a fact: Sandberg's parents saw Duren pitch in Milwaukee and named their second-born son after him.]

—RYNE DUREN

"I think Casey would have liked Ozzie Smith—a defensive player first who thinks before a play happens. He would have reminded Casey of Nellie Fox. He would have liked Robin Yount, too. Robin is the kind of player who takes the extra base and doesn't make mistakes. That's why he's been MVP.

"Of course, Yount is also a repositioned shortstop. Casey liked shortstops who could move to other positions. DiMaggio and Mantle started there."

—TONY KUBEK

"I think Casey would have liked Don Mattingly and Rickey Henderson. Mattingly's a good all-around hitter and Henderson, of course, is a great basestealer. The Yankees under Stengel never had that kind of speed."

—EDDIE LOPAT

"I think he'd like Brook Jacoby. He's a throwback: He comes to play and doesn't get headaches in his fingernails. What is this twenty-one-day disabled list? If you got out of the line-up with the Yankees, you could forget about it."

—GENE WOODLING

"Today? Casey would like aggressive overachievers like Kirby Puckett and Kevin Mitchell—guys who hit the ball all over the park without being particularly stylish."

—MAURY ALLEN

"Casey liked a guy you can write in the line-up every day and turn loose, not guys who played four days a week. His modern favorites would be players like Pete Rose and Lenny Dykstra."

—RICHIE ASHBURN

"Darrell Porter. I had five winning teams in eight years with him. He was an outstanding baserunner and he could always hit behind the runner and advance them two bases. Casey also liked Roger Maris, who could pull the ball, play defense, and throw well. He would have called Ozzie Smith 'my Rizzuto.' Of course, Casey really liked bigger shortstops, like Tony Kubek. He said they could catch line drives better than the little guys."

—WHITEY HERZOG

"Casey would like Mike Scott in his prime. He'd want him going in the big games. He'd love Ozzie, because he made himself into a better player by hitting for a higher average. He'd like Rick Reuschel, because he'd want to relieve the day after he got rocked. All Casey ever wanted to do was win."

—SOLLY HEMUS

10

Mister Stengel Goes to Washington

ON JULY 9, 1958, Casey was called to Washington to testify before the Subcommittee on Antitrust and Monopoly of the Committee of the Judiciary of the United States Senate. The committee was considering a bill to exempt professional baseball, basketball, football and hockey from the antitrust laws. Some consider Casey's testimony, which is excerpted below, to be his finest hour.

SEN. ESTES KEFAUVER: Mr. Stengel, you are the manager of the New York Yankees. Will you give us very briefly your background and your views about this legislation?

STENGEL: Well, I started in professional ball in 1910. I have been in professional ball, I would say, for forty-eight years. I have been employed by numerous ball clubs in the majors and in the minor leagues.

I started in the minors with Kansas City. I played as low as Class D ball, which was in Shelbyville, Kentucky, and also Class C ball and Class A ball, and I have advanced in baseball as a ballplayer.

I had many years that I was not so successful as a ballplayer, as it is a game of skill. And then I was no doubt discharged by baseball in which I had to go back to the minor leagues as a manager, and after being in the minor leagues as a manager, I became a major-league manager in several cities and was discharged, we call it discharged, because there is no question I had to leave.

And I returned to the minor leagues at Milwaukee, Kansas City and Oakland, California, and then returned to the major leagues.

In the last ten years, naturally, in major-league baseball with the New York Yankees; the New York Yankees have had tremendous success, and while I am not a ballplayer who does the work, I have no doubt worked for a ball club that is very capable in the office.

I have been up and down the ladder. I know there are some things in baseball thirty-five to fifty years ago that are better now than they were in those days. In those days, my goodness, you could not transfer a ball club in the minor leagues. Class D, Class C ball, Class A ball.

How could you transfer a ball club when you did not have a highway? How could you transfer a ball club when the railroad then would take you to a town, you got off and then you had to wait and sit up five hours to go to another ball club?

How could you run baseball then without night ball?

You had to have night ball to improve the proceeds, to pay larger salaries, and I went to work, the first year I received $135 a month.

I thought that was amazing. I had to put away enough money to go to dental college. I found out it was not better in dentistry. I stayed in baseball. Any other question you would like to ask me?

SEN. KEFAUVER: Mr. Stengel are you prepared to answer particularly why baseball wants this bill passed?

STENGEL: Well, I would have to say at the present time, I think that baseball has advanced in this respect for the player help. This is an amazing statement for me to make, because you can retire with an annuity at fifty, and what organization in America allows you to retire at fifty and make money?

I want to further state that I am not a ballplayer, that is, put into that pension fund committee. At my age, and I have been in baseball, well, I will say I am possibly the oldest man who is working in baseball. I would say that when they start an annuity for the ballplayers to better their conditions, it should have been done, and I think it has been done.

I think it should be the way they have done it, which is a very good thing.

The reason they possibly did not take the managers in at that time was because radio and television or the income to ball clubs was not large enough that you could have put in a pension plan.

Now I am not a member of the pension plan. You have young men here who are, who represent the ball clubs.

They represent the players, and since I am not a member and don't receive pension from a fund which you think, my goodness, he ought to be declared in that, too, but I would say that is a great thing for the ballplayers.

That is one thing I will say for the ballplayers, they have an advanced pension fund. I should think it was gained by radio and television or you could not have enough money to pay anything of that type.

Now the second thing about baseball that I think is very interesting to the public or to all of us that it is the owner's own fault if he does not improve his club, along with the officials in the ball club and the players.

Now what causes that?

If I am going to go on the road and we are a traveling ball club and you know the cost of transportation now—we travel sometimes with three Pullman coaches, the New York Yankees and remember that I am just a salaried man, and do not own stock in the New York Yankees, I found out that in traveling with the New York Yankees on the road and all, that it is the best, and we have broken records in Washington this year, we have broken them in every city but New York and we have lost two clubs that have gone out of the city of New York.

Of course, we have had some bad weather, I would say that they are mad at us in Chicago, we fill the parks.

They have come out to see good material. I will say that they are mad at us in Kansas City, but we broke their attendance record.

Now on the road we only get possibly twenty-seven cents. I am not positive of these figures, as I am not an official.

If you go back fifteen years or so if I owned stock in the club, I would give them to you.

SEN. KEFAUVER: Mr. Stengel, I am not sure that I made my question clear.

STENGEL: Yes, sir. Well, that is all right. I am not sure I am going to answer yours perfectly, either.

SEN. JOSEPH C. O'MAHONEY: How many minor leagues were there in baseball when you began?

STENGEL: Well, there were not so many at that time because of this fact: Anybody to go into baseball at that time with the educational schools that we had were small, while you were probably thoroughly educated at school, you had to be—we only had small cities that you could put up a team in and they would go defunct.

Why, I remember the first year that I was at Kankakee, Illinois, and a bank offered me $550 if I would let them have a little notice. I left there and took a uniform because they owed me two weeks' pay. But I either had to quit but I did not have enough money to go to dental college so I had to go with the manager down to Kentucky.

What happened there was if you got by July, that was the big date. You did not play night ball and you did not play Sundays in half the cities on account of a Sunday observance, so in those days when things were tough, and all of it was, I mean to say, why they just closed up July 4 and there you were sitting in the depot.

You could go to work someplace else, but that was it.

So I got out of Kankakee, Illinois, and I just go there for the visit now.

SEN. JOHN A. CARROLL: The question Senator Kefauver asked you was what, in your honest opinion, with your forty-eight years of experience, is the need for this legislation in view of the fact that baseball has not been subject to antitrust laws?

STENGEL: No.

SEN. WILLIAM LANGER: Mr. Chairman, my final question. This is the Antimonopoly Committee that has been sitting here.

STENGEL: Yes, sir.

SEN. LANGER: I want to know whether you intend to keep on monopolizing the world's championship in New York City.

STENGEL: Well, I will tell you. I got a little concern yesterday in the first three innings when I saw the three players I had gotten rid of, and I said when I lost nine what am I going to do and when I had a couple of my players. I thought so great of that did not do so good up to the sixth inning I was more confused but I finally had to go and call on a young man from Baltimore that we don't own and the Yankees don't own him, and he is doing pretty good, and I would actually have to tell you that I think we are more the Greta Garbo type now from success.

We are being hated, I mean, from the ownership and all, we are being hated. Every sport that gets too great or one individual—but if we made twenty-seven cents and it pays to have a winner at home, why would you not have a good winner in your own park if you were an owner?

That is the result of baseball. An owner gets most of the money at home and it is up to him and his staff to do better or they ought to be discharged.

SEN. KEFAUVER: Thank you very much, Mr. Stengel. We appreciate your presence here.

Mr. Mickey Mantle, will you come around? . . . Mr. Mantle, do you have any observations with reference to the applicability of the antitrust laws to baseball?

MANTLE: My views are just about the same as Casey's.

AFTERWORD

Following a long illness, Casey Stengel died in Glendale, California, on September 29, 1975, at age eighty-five. "Well," wrote columnist Jim Murray, "God is getting an earful tonight."

(NBL)

DRAMATIS PERSONAE

(WHEN QUOTED WITHOUT IDENTIFICATION)

Maury Allen—Longtime baseball writer and Stengel biographer.

Sparky Anderson—Detroit Tigers manager.

Richie Ashburn—Hall-of-fame-calibre outfielder who finished career with Mets.

Hank Bauer—Former Baltimore manager and Yankee outfielder.

Larry Bearnarth—Colorado Rockies executive and former Montreal pitching coach and Mets pitcher.

Yogi Berra—Hall-of-Fame Yankee catcher.

Johnny Blanchard—Former Yankee utility man.

Frenchy Bordagaray—Outfielder under Stengel with Dodgers.

Clete Boyer—Former Yankee third baseman.

Bobby Bragan—Former manager.

Bobby Brown—American League president and former Yankee infielder.

Tom Callahan—Columnist for *U.S. News & World Report* and the *Washington Post.*

Roy Campanella, Jr.—Son of the Hall-of-Fame catcher.

Andy Carey—Former Yankee infielder.

Roger Craig—Giants manager and former Mets pitcher.

Robert W. Creamer—Special contributor to *Sports Illustrated* and author of *Stengel: His Life and Times.*

Frank Crosetti—Former Yankee coach.

Arthur Daley—Late Pulitzer Prize–winning *New York Times* sports columnist.

Ryne Duren—Former Yankee pitcher.

Harry Eisenstadt—Dodger pitcher under Casey.

Bob Fishel—Late Yankee publicist and assistant to the American League president.

Whitey Ford—Hall-of-Fame Yankee pitcher.

Jesse Gonder—Former Mets catcher.

Bert Gordon—Detroit Tiger fan who was profiled by Roger Angell in *The New Yorker.*

Solly Hemus—Former Mets coach.

Tommy Hensich—Former Yankee.

Whitey Herzog—Former manager and Yankee farmhand.

Ralph Houk—Former manager and Yankee catcher.

Elston Howard—Late Hall-of-Fame catcher and first black Yankee.

Ron Hunt—Former Mets second baseman.

Alvin Jackson—Former Oriole pitching coach and former Mets pitcher.

Rod Kanehl—Former Mets jack-of-all-trades.

Larry King—Radio and television interviewer.

Ed Kranepool—Former Mets first baseman/outfielder.

Tony Kubek—Broadcaster and former Yankee shortstop.

Johnny Kucks—Former Yankee pitcher.

Jack Lang—Sportswriter.

Ring Lardner—The late novelist and sports columnist.

Edward Lian—Sportswriter.

Eddie Lopat—Former Yankee pitcher.

Al Lopez—Hall-of-Famer who caught for Stengel in Brooklyn and managed against him with the Indians and White Sox.

Lee MacPhail—Former Yankee executive and American League president.

Ken MacKenzie—Former Mets pitcher.

Mickey Mantle—Hall-of-Fame Yankee center fielder.

Gil McDougald—Former Yankee infielder.

Sam Malc—Former Minnesota manager.

Tom Owens—Collector of sports memorabilia.

Harry T. Paxton—Co-author of Casey's autobiography, *Casey at the Bat.*

Joe Page—Former Yankee reliever.

Joe Pignatano—Dodger coach and former Mets catcher.

Vic Power—One of the greatest righthanded-fielding first basemen; played for seven teams in 1954–65.

Allie Reynolds—Former Yankee pitcher.

Bobby Richardson—Former Yankee second baseman.

Phil Rizzuto—Broadcaster and former Yankee shortstop.

Ed Roebuck—Former Dodger pitcher.

Harold Rosenthal—Retired New York City sportswriter.

Johnny Sain—Former Yankee pitcher and well-traveled pitching coach.

Leonard Schecter—Late author and New York City sports columnist.

Norm Sherry—Former Giants pitching coach and Mets catcher.

Sibby Sisti—Utility man who played for Stengel with the Braves.

Moose Skowron—Former Yankee first baseman.

Enos Slaughter—Hall-of-Fame outfielder who finished his career with the Yankees.

Red Smith—Late Pulitzer Prize–winning *New York Times* sports columnist.

Warren Spahn—Hall-of-Fame pitcher who played for Casey with the Braves and Mets.

Ron Swoboda—Former Mets outfielder.

Marv Throneberry—Former Mets first baseman.

Jim Turner—Casey's pitching coach with the Yankees. Also pitched for him with the Braves and managed against him in the minors.

Joe Williams—Late New York City sports columnist.

Ted Williams—Hall-of-Fame Red Sox left fielder.

Gene Woodling—Former Yankee outfielder.

Don Zimmer—Red Sox coach and former Cubs manager and former Mets infielder.

CHRONOLOGY

CHARLES DILLON STENGEL

Born at Kansas City, Mo., July 30, 1890 • Died in Glendale, Cal., September 29, 1975
Height, 5'10". • Weight, 175. • Batted and threw left.
Elected to Hall of Fame in 1966.

RECORD AS A PLAYER

YEAR	TEAM & LEAGUE	G	AB	R	H	2b	3b	HR	RBI	AVG.
1910	Kankakee, N.A.	59	203	27	51	7	1	1		.251
1910	Maysville, Bl.Gr.	69	233	27	52	10	5	2		.352
1911	Aurora, Wis.-Ill.	121	420	76	148	23	6	4		.352
1912	Montgomery, S.A.	136	479	85	139					.290
1912	Brooklyn, N.L.	17	57	9	18	1	0	1	13	.316
1913	Brooklyn, N.L.	124	438	60	119	16	8	7	43	.272
1914	Brooklyn, N.L.	126	412	55	130	13	10	4	60	.316
1915	Brooklyn, N.L.	132	459	52	109	20	12	3	50	.237
1916	Brooklyn, N.L.	127	462	66	129	27	8	8	53	.279
1917	Brooklyn, N.L.	150	549	69	141	23	12	6	73	.257
1918	Pittsburgh, N.L.	39	122	18	30	4	1	1	12	.246
1919	Pittsburgh, N.L.	89	321	38	94	10	10	4	43	.293
1920	Philadelphia, N.L.	129	445	53	130	25	6	9	50	.292
1921	Phila.-N.Y., N.L.	42	81	11	23	4	1	0	6	.284
1922	New York, N.L.	84	250	48	92	8	10	7	48	.368
1923	New York, N.L.	75	218	39	74	11	5	5	43	.339
1924	Boston, N.L.	131	461	57	129	20	6	5	39	.280
1925	Boston, N.L.	12	13	0	1	0	0	0	2	.077
1925	Worcester, E.L.	100	334	73	107	27	2	10		.320
1926	Toledo, A.A.	88	201	40	66	14	2	0	27	.328
1927	Toledo, A.A.	18	17	3	3	0	0	1	3	.176
1928	Toledo, A.A.	26	32	5	14	5	0	0	12	.438
1929	Toledo, A.A.	20	31	2	7	1	1	0	9	.226
1931	Toledo, A.A.	2	8	1	3	2	0	0	0	.375

Major league totals	1277	4288	575	1219	182	89	60	535	.284

N.A.	—	Northern Association		N.L.	—	National League	
Bl.Gr.	—	Blue Grass League		E.L.	—	Eastern League	
Wis.-Ill.	—	Wisconsin-Illinois League		A.A.	—	American Association	
S.A.	—	Southern Association					

WORLD SERIES RECORD

YEAR	TEAM	G	AB	R	H	2b	3b	HR	RBI	AVG.
1916	Brooklyn	4	11	2	4	0	0	0	0	.364
1922	New York	2	5	0	2	0	0	0	0	.400
1923	New York	6	12	3	5	0	0	2	4	.417
	World Series Totals	12	20	5	11	0	0	2	4	.393

RECORD AS A MANAGER

YEAR	CLUB & LEAGUE	FINISHED	WON	LOST	PCT.
1925	Worcester, E.L.	3	70	55	.560
1926	Toledo, A.A.	4	87	77	.530
1927	Toledo, A.A.	1	101	67	.601
1928	Toledo, A.A.	6	79	88	.473
1929	Toledo, A.A.	8	67	100	.401
1930	Toledo, A.A.	3	88	66	.571
1931	Toledo, A.A.	8	68	100	.405
1934	Brooklyn, N.L.	6	71	81	.467
1935	Brooklyn, N.L.	5	70	83	.458
1936	Brooklyn, N.L.	7	67	87	.435
1938	Boston, N.L.	5	77	75	.507
1939	Boston, N.L.	7	63	88	.417
1940	Boston, N.L.	7	65	87	.428
1941	Boston, N.L.	7	62	92	.403
1942	Boston, N.L.	7	59	89	.399
1943	Boston, N.L.	6	68	85	.439
1944	Milwaukee, A.A.	1	91	49	.650
1945	Kansas City, A.A.	7	65	86	.430
1946	Oakland, P.C.L.	2	111	72	.607
1947	Oakland, P.C.L.	4	96	90	.516
1948	Oakland, P.C.L.	1	114	74	.606
1949	New York, A.L.*	1	97	57	.630
1950	New York, A.L.*	1	98	56	.636

1951	New York, A.L.*	1	98	56	.636
1952	New York, A.L.*	1	95	59	.617
1953	New York, A.L.*	1	99	52	.656
1954	New York, A.L.	2	103	51	.669
1955	New York, A.L.	1	96	58	.623
1956	New York, A.L.*	1	97	57	.630
1957	New York, A.L.	1	98	56	.636
1958	New York, A.L.*	1	92	62	.597
1959	New York, A.L.	3	79	75	.513
1960	New York, A.L.	1	97	57	.630
1962	New York, N.L.	10	40	120	.250
1963	New York, N.L.	10	51	111	.315
1964	New York, N.L.	10	53	109	.327
1965	New York, N.L.	—	31	64	.326
25 years: Major league totals		—	1905	1842	.508

E.L.	—	Eastern League	P.C.L.	—	Pacific Coast League
A.A.	—	American Association	A.L.	—	American League
N.L.	—	National League	N.L.	—	National League

*Won World Series.

WORLD SERIES RECORD

YEAR	WON	LOST	PCT.
1949	4	1	.800
1950	4	0	1.000
1951	4	2	.667
1952	4	3	.571
1953	4	2	.667
1955	3	4	.429
1956	4	3	.571
1957	3	4	.429
1958	4	3	.571
1960	3	4	.429
10 YEARS:	37	26	.587

SELECTED SOURCES

BOOKS

A Thinking Man's Guide to Baseball, by Leonard Koppett
Baseball Anecdotes, by Daniel Okrent and Steve Wulf
Baseball from a Different Angle, by Bob Broeg
Baseball History 3, edited by Peter Levine
Baseball's Great Experiment, by Jules Tygiel
Baseball's Greatest Managers, by Edwin Pope
Baseball's Greatest Quotations, by Paul Dickson
Beyond the Dream, by Ira Berkow
Blackball Stars, by John B. Holway
Can't Anybody Here Play This Game?, by Jimmy Breslin
Casey & Mr. McGraw, by Joseph Durso
Casey at the Bat: The Story of My Life in Baseball, by Casey Stengel as told
    to Harry T. Paxton
Casey Stengel, by Frank Graham
Casey: The Life and Legend of Charles Dillon Stengel, by Joseph Durso
Casey's Secret, by Clay Felker
Jackie Robinson: A Life Remembered, by Maury Allen
Men at Work, by George F. Will
Now Wait a Minute, Casey, by Maury Allen
Number 1, by Billy Martin and Peter Golenbock
Stengel: His Life and Times, by Robert W. Creamer
Summer of '49, by David Halberstam
The Education of a Baseball Player, by Mickey Mantle
The Fireside Book of Baseball (18th edition)
The Jocks, by Leonard Schecter
The Joe Williams Reader, edited by Peter Williams
The New York Times Book of Sports Legends, edited by Joseph Vecchione

White Rat, by Whitey Herzog
You Could Look It Up: The Life of Casey Stengel, by Maury Allen

MAGAZINE ARTICLES

"Baseball's Grand Old Man," by Elston Howard, *Reader's Digest*, Oct. 1967

"Can't Anybody Here Play This Game?," by Jimmy Breslin, *Reader's Digest*, Aug. 1963

"Casey Stengel," by Bill James, *Sport*, Dec. 1986

"Casey Stengel—an Appreciation," by Robert W. Creamer, *Sports Illustrated*, Oct. 13, 1975

"Casey Stengel: The Ole Professor Still Wields Profound Influence," by Jim Kaplan, Historical Perspective department, *The Show*, Spring 1991

"Casey the Indestructible," by Harry T. Paxton, *The Saturday Evening Post*, April 7, 1962

"Exit the Genius-Clown," *Time*, Sept. 10, 1965

"Musings of a Dugout Socrates," by Gilbert Millstein, *The New York Times Magazine*, 1963

"Remembering Casey," by Kenneth MacKenzie, *The Yale Review*, Winter 1987

"The Improbable Casey Stengel," by John Lardner, *Sport*, Dec. 1948

"The Last Angry Man," by Edward Linn, *The Saturday Evening Post*, July 3, 1965

"They Didn't Hire Him for Laughs," by Tom Meany, *The Saturday Evening Post*, March 12, 1949

"Was Casey Really So Great?," by Leslie Lieber, *This Week* magazine, three-part series starting June 25, 1961

NEWSPAPER ARTICLES

"A Man for Many Seasons," by John Vergara, *New York Sunday News*, July 24, 1966

"Bees' Tough Luck Sharpens Stengel's Stinging Wit; Merry Manager Even Able to Joke Over Injury Jinx," by Howell Stevens of the *Boston Post*, *The Sporting News*, Dec. 28, 1939

"Casey Comes Back," by Richards Vidmer, *New York Tribune*, Oct. 27, 1937

"Casey Is Still as Baffling as Ever," by Ira Berkow, Newspaper Enterprise Association, Sept. 14, 1976

"Casey Pioneer as Designator," by Milton Richman, United Press International, *Boston Globe*, Jan. 16, 1973

"Casey Stengel Lives," by George Vecsey, *New York Times*, Sept. 18, 1987

"Celebrating Casey's 100th," by Steve Jacobson, *Newsday*, Aug. 26, 1990

"Day Nursery," by Red Smith, *New York Herald Tribune*, Oct. 8, 1950

"Drama in Stengelese: You Can Look It Up," by Ira Berkow, *New York Times*, April 15, 1981

"Interim Report on the Yankees," by Arthur Daley, *New York Times*, March 16, 1949

"I Remember Casey," by Bill Gallo, *New York Daily News*, April 19, 1987

"Last Time Around for Casey," by Red Smith, *New York Times*, Oct. 7, 1975

"Stengel's Death at 85 Widely Mourned," by Joseph Durso, *New York Times*, Oct. 1, 1975

"Stengel Still a Man for All Seasons," by Jerome Holtzman, *Chicago Tribune*, Aug. 5, 1990

"The Amazing Met," by Bob Sales, *New York Herald Tribune*, March 28, 1965

"The Best of Casey Stengel," by George Vecsey, *Newsday*, Aug. 31, 1965

"The Lefthanded Dentist: 84 and Still Talking," by John Hall of the *Los Angeles Times*, *New York Post*, July 31, 1974

"The Ol' Perfesser Taught in a Language, Style All His Own," by Eliot Cohen, *Washington Post*, July 30, 1990

"They've All Got Automobiles," by Casey Stengel, *New York Times*, Oct. 9, 1970

"When Casey Buried, the Laughs Go with Him," by Dick Young, *New York Daily News*, Oct. 5, 1975

"Yankees Fired Casey for Being 70 . . . Mets Hired Him Because He Was 70," by Maury Allen, *New York Post*, July 30, 1975

INTERVIEWS

Maury Allen, Sparky Anderson, Richie Ashburn, Hank Bauer, Larry Bearnarth, Yogi Berra, John Blanchard, Frenchy Bordagaray, Bobby Brown, Tom Callahan, Andy Carey, Bob Case, Roger Craig, Robert W. Creamer, Frank Crosetti, Ryne Duren, Harry Eisenstadt, Whitey Ford, Jesse Gonder, Solly Hemus, Tommy Henrich, Whitey Herzog, Ralph Houk, Ron Hunt, Alvin Jackson, Rod Kanehl, Ed Kranepool, Tony Kubek, Johnny Kucks, Jack Lang, Eddie Lopat, Al Lopez, Mickey

Mantle, Joe Pignatano, Allie Reynolds, Johnny Sain, Norm Sherry, Sibby Sisti, Moose Skowron, Enos Slaughter, Ron Swoboda, Marv Throneberry, Jim Turner, Don Zimmer

CORRESPONDENCE

Jay Feldman, Bert Gordon, Jack Kavanagh, Gil McDougald, Jeffrey H. Orleans, Tom Owens, Peter Williams.